FORTY YEARS
OF THE PUBLIC SCHOOLS
IN MISSISSIPPI

WITH SPECIAL REFERENCE TO THE
EDUCATION OF THE NEGRO

By

STUART GRAYSON NOBLE, PH.D.

Professor of Education in Millsaps College

NEGRO UNIVERSITIES PRESS
NEW YORK

Originally published in 1918
by the Teachers College, Columbia University

Reprinted 1969 by
Negro Universities Press
A DIVISION OF GREENWOOD PUBLISHING CORP.
NEW YORK

SBN 8371-1939-1

PRINTED IN UNITED STATES OF AMERICA

PREFACE

In the babel of many voices arising in the South, it is difficult at times to determine just what is the attitude of the southern white people toward the education of the Negro. It is frequently asked: Do southern people believe that the Negro can and should be educated? What facilities have been provided for this purpose? Is the trend of public sentiment toward providing more adequate means for his education? Is the Negro child being discriminated against in the distribution of school funds? Does the progress of the race in the past fifty years justify the efforts that have been put forth to educate the Negro?

In an effort to answer these questions the author has undertaken to trace the history of public education in the typically southern state of Mississippi, taking pains at every stage in the progress of the narrative to inquire what southern white people have thought and done about the education of the Negro. I have studied closely the social and economic conditions of the state during the forty years between 1870 and 1910, and have sought the bearing of these conditions upon the education of both white and colored races. In this study, since practically nothing has been done along this line in Mississippi, I have been forced to draw my conclusions largely from data contained in the state records, in the government reports, and in a limited number of local newspapers.

This study was begun during the summer of 1915 in a course in the History of Education in the United States, conducted by Dr. Paul Monroe in Teachers College, Columbia University. I am under special obligation to Dr. Monroe for his wise and helpful suggestions as to the plan and purpose of the study.

I wish to acknowledge the valuable assistance of the Faculty committee which examined it, Dr. William H. Kilpatrick and Dr. David Snedden. I am also under obligations to Dr. Dunbar Rowland, director of the Department of Archives and History of Mississippi; to Dr. J. C. Fant, of the University of Mississippi; to

Professor E. C. Branson, of the University of North Carolina; to Mr. Jackson Davis, field agent of the General Education Board; and to my colleagues, Dr. A. A. Kern and Dr. J. M. Burton, of Millsaps College, for reading the manuscript and offering suggestions for its improvement.

S. G. N.

TABLE OF CONTENTS

CHAPTER I

THE SOCIAL AND ECONOMIC SETTING, 1870–1871

Introductory. In its legal status the public school system of Mississippi is not, nor has it ever been, a dual system. There is a single school system which provides educational advantages for the children of both races. If there were a legal provision which specifically prohibited the children of one race from enjoying the school privileges extended to the other, such a provision would be rendered null and void by the Federal Constitution, as a discrimination based upon "race, color, or previous condition of servitude." The history of the public schools is therefore not the history of the schools which the state has provided for the instruction of the white youth, but the history of schools provided for the instruction of both races. Despite, however, the equal status before the law of white and colored schools, educational facilities for the colored race have not run parallel with those provided for the whites. Recognizing this difference the author, although he is particularly interested in tracing the development of education for Negroes, is forced to give a comprehensive treatment of the public school system with respect to the education of both races, in order to give a faithful account of the Negro schools.

Economic and social conditions that have tended to promote the growth and efficiency of the public school system have in large measure affected the trend of Negro education. In like manner, efficiency, or lack of efficiency, in the administration of education has been felt in both white and colored schools. At the beginning of this study, therefore, it would be well to give an account not only of the organization of the public school system, but to take into consideration the social and economic conditions which attended its birth.

Density of Population. Density of population is an important factor in determining the growth and efficiency of school systems. To what extent this factor was influential at this period in Mississippi, we may learn from a study of the census reports of 1870.

There were then, according to the census returns, 382,896 whites and 444,201 Negroes, distributed over an area of 46,810 square miles, or 17.9 persons to the square mile. An idea of the relative density of the state may be had if we consider that the density of Ohio [1] at this time was 65.4; of Pennsylvania, 78.3; of New York, 92.0; and of Massachusetts, 181.3. There were only two [2] counties in the state with a population over 30,000, and there were seven counties [3] with less than 5,000. There were only four towns in the state with a population over 2,000, and Vicksburg, the largest of these, had only 12,443.

The importance of density of population with respect to education may be seen in the following statements. In fifteen counties, comprising an area of 9,292 square miles, the Negroes out-numbered the whites nearly three to one.[4] In this 'black belt' there were 179,237 Negroes and 60,004 whites, or 298 Negroes to every 100 whites. This situation was equalled in only one other southern state, Alabama, which had a somewhat more extensive black belt with 315 Negroes to every 100 whites. The black belt counties of Mississippi were among the most populous of the state, and yet there were but 19.3 Negroes and 5.1 whites to the square mile. This means that even the most populous areas of the state were but sparsely settled. It means, further, if we allow three children to the family, that there were many townships in this section in which thirty-six white families [5] would have to support schools for approximately 100 white children and 400 Negro children. But educational conditions were more favorable, under a system of local taxation, in the black belt than in many of the more sparsely settled white counties, since the black counties were not only the most populous but the richest. In respect to the poor white counties Superintendent Pease reported [6] in 1872 that there were many in which the

---

[1] I refer to these states in particular because many of the northern men who had in hand the organization of the new school system, were most familiar with schools in these states, and hoped to plant their old ideas in new soil. They failed to consider the difference pointed out above.

[2] Hinds and Lowndes.

[3] The 'white counties': Greene, Hancock, Jackson, Jones, Marion, Wayne, Perry.

[4] Kelley Miller: *Education of the Negro*, United States Commissioner's Report, 1900–1901, p. 731.

[5] The white families were the tax-payers; the Negroes had not yet acquired property to any extent.

[6] United States Commissioner's Report, 1873, p. 213.

maximum tax levy (ten mills for schoolhouses and five for teachers) would not raise revenue sufficient to educate one-fourth of the scholastic population. It is clear, therefore, that the factor of sparse distribution of the population was to play an important part in determining the number, size, and grade of schools to be established, as well as in determining their future support.

Illiteracy. The problem of illiteracy in 1870 was not complicated to an undue extent by the question of race. It was mainly a colored problem. Advance sheets of the census [7] this year showed that out of a total population of 382,896 whites, there were 23,103 adult illiterates; and that out of a total of 444,896 Negroes, there were 168,031 adult illiterates. It is evident that very few adult Negroes were able to read and write. These figures are sufficient to indicate that the educational problem in 1870 was largely the problem of providing schools for Negroes for whom no schools had heretofore existed.

Economic Situation. The economic situation has much to do in shaping the sentiment of people toward education. A brief summary therefore will not be out of place just here. The following figures represent the assessed value of real and personal property for the years indicated: [8]

1860	$509,472,902
1865	134,131,128
1870	177,288,892

It is impossible to estimate the market value of this property, but considering the unsettled times, the figures for 1865 and 1870 are certainly not underestimated. It may be added that during the decade between 1860 and 1870 the value of farm property [9] alone declined from $241,478,571 to $92,890,758, or 61.5 per cent. During the same period the cotton crop declined from 1,202,507 bales to 565,559. The demoralization of war and the inability to make a proper adjustment to the new economic situation are written large in these figures.

An element worthy of consideration in this connection is the fact that the cotton crops for 1866, 1867, and 1870 were failures.

---

[7] United States Commissioner's Report, 1871, p. 68.

[8] United States Congress, Report of Committee on Affairs in Late Insurrectionary States, p. 179.

[9] Abstract of United States Census, 1910, Mississippi Supplement, p. 612.

In addition to this, levees (embankments) which had protected the fertile Yazoo Valley, and which had been cut during the war, were not repaired until 1870. This threw open to the floods 4,000,000 acres of the most fertile land in the state.[10]

Still another factor which contributed to the general demoralization was the fact that the state had suffered the loss of nearly $8,000,000 worth of cotton by confiscation, and the loss by conflagration during the war of countless numbers of courthouses and public buildings. The Federal government also had levied a two-and-one-half-mill tax upon every pound of cotton for the years 1866 and 1867, and a three-mill tax for 1868.[11]

To complete the story of demoralization we may add the difficulty of controlling labor in this unsettled period of readjustment, and the inability of both races readily to adapt themselves to the new situation.

Such was the economic situation in 1870 when it was proposed to establish a system of public schools, costing $1,000,000 for equipment, and $400,000 annually for maintenance.[12] The initial cost was particularly heavy because of the necessity of establishing separate schools for whites and blacks. The white tax-payers, already driven to the verge of bankruptcy by the excessive burdens of war and taxation, were called upon to support this new burden.

The Political Situation, 1865–1870. A brief review of the political situation is in order just here that we may understand the circumstances under which the public school system was organized. Immediately after the close of the Civil War, Governor Clark was arrested by the federal authorities and placed in prison, and Judge William L. Sharkey was appointed by President Johnson as provisional governor. Judge Sharkey, an esteemed citizen of the state, shortly after assuming the duties of governor, called a convention for the purpose of revising the constitution, with a view to making it conform to the federal requirements. The convention met in 1865, but the changes which were made in the constitution failed to satisfy the United States government. The members of the convention were representative Southerners and naturally their views on Negro suffrage and the new status of the freedman

[10] Garner: *Reconstruction in Mississippi*, Chap. IV.
[11] *Ibid.*
[12] The estimate of Governor Alcorn here given is doubtless conservative. See Message on Education, 1870, House Journal, Appendix, p. 12.

did not coincide with northern views. The instrument, however, was accepted by the state, an election was held by the southern white citizens, and the legislature was called to adapt the old code to the new social situation. General B. G. Humphreys, a prominent Mississippian, was elected governor.

Meanwhile, a federal military governor exercised police control in the state, his authority at times conflicting with that of the civil authorities. As soon as the constitution of 1865 was rejected by the federal government the military governor began organizing the new electorate for the purpose of selecting delegates to a second Constitutional Convention. In 1868 the military governor saw fit to exercise his legal prerogative of removing the civil governor, General Humphreys, and to appoint in his place General Adelbert Ames, of the federal army.

Under the leadership of military authorities, Freedmen's Bureau officials, and carpet-baggers, the Negroes were organized into the Republican party, and when the election of delegates to the Constitutional Convention took place, the Republicans returned a substantial majority. Of the hundred delegates, seventeen were Negroes, some twenty or more were carpet-baggers, and twenty-nine were 'scalawags'. Altogether it was a motley gathering that constituted what became known as the 'Black and Tan Convention'.

The constitution drafted by this body proved acceptable alike to the federal government and to the new proletariat of Mississippi. It was ratified in 1869; state officers were elected under its provisions in the fall of the same year. The Republicans found themselves masters of the situation, with a good majority in the legislature. General A. L. Alcorn, a Southerner who believed in pursuing a policy of conciliation with the new proletariat, was elected governor. Captain H. R. Pease, then at the head of the Freedmen's Bureau schools in the state, became superintendent of education.[13]

[13] The historical information included in this section has been derived mainly from Garner's *Reconstruction in Mississippi* and from McNeily's *Provisional Government of Mississippi*.

CHAPTER II

THE ATTITUDE OF THE SEVERAL SOCIAL ELEMENTS
TOWARD NEGRO EDUCATION

The Attitude of Southern Whites before 1870. The best element of southern citizenry were quick to realize in the passing of the Negro from slavery into freedom, that the necessity of educating him to fit into the new social fabric stared them in the face. Although many seriously doubted his ability to profit from schooling beyond certain limits, there seems to have been a very general disposition among southern white people to provide schools for his instruction. We find evidences of this attitude as early as 1865.

In the inaugural address of Governor Humphreys, October 16, 1865, we find this statement:[1] "The highest degree of elevation in the scale of civilization to which they are capable, morally and intellectually, must be secured to them by their education and religious training." The governor expressed his faith by works when, in 1867, he established a Freedmen's Bureau school upon his own plantation.[2]

General Thomas J. Wood, assistant commissioner of the Freedmen's Bureau, in the fall of 1866 attempted to enlist the coöperation of the white citizens of the state in the establishment of a system of Negro schools. His proposition was endorsed by clergymen and bishops of the various denominations, and seems to have been quite generally approved throughout the state.[3] Dr. C. K. Marshall, a prominent clergyman of the day, was one of the most enthusiastic supporters of the plan. In an address published in December, 1866, he strongly expressed this opinion: "The education of the freedmen's children in the common branches taught in our schools, is unquestionably a duty we owe alike to ourselves and to them." Early in 1867, J. M. Langston made a tour of the state in the inter-

---

[1] Governor Humphreys was elected by the southern whites in 1865. He was a typical representative of the Old South. See McNeily: *Provisional Government of Mississippi*, Publications, Mississippi Historical Society, 1916, p. 16.

[2] Freedmen's Bureau Report, January 1, 1867, p. 17.

[3] McNeily: *Provisional Government of Mississippi*, p. 237.

est of the Freedmen's Bureau, and reported as follows: "I talked with no leading influential white man in Mississippi, whatever may have been his views with regard to the late rebellion and the abolition of slavery, who did not express the opinion, apparently with full earnestness, that the freedmen ought to be educated."

On January 17, 1867, at the organization meeting of the State Teachers' Association,[4] the representative southern white teachers went on record as favoring a state system of public schools for white and colored children alike. The resolution which embodies their opinion reads:

Resolved, 1. That the enactment of a public school system that shall meet the wants and necessities of the entire population is a desideratum of the utmost importance.

2. That it is the duty as well as the interest of the state, through its legislature, to establish and maintain normal schools in different parts of the state for the purpose of educating colored teachers, so that they may be qualified to labor as teachers among the colored population of the state.

3. That it would be for the interest of the people and the promotion of education to have a uniform system.

A year later, the platform of the Democratic State Convention contained the following resolution:[5]

Resolved . . . that we will in good faith and willingly aid in securing to the colored race the security of person and property, and full guarantees against oppression and injustice as freedmen; cherishing against them no feeling of hostility, and desiring that they may elevate themselves in the scale of humanity by mental culture to any extent of which they may be capable.

While there seems to have been little objection to the education of the Negro, there was objection to the means by which it was being undertaken. Numerous citations may be noted which indicate hostility to northern teachers and to northern doctrines. The Jackson *Standard* voices objection in these words:[6]

We are glad to see an awakening disposition on the part of the southern people to take charge of schools for little Negroes, and have them taught by southern teachers instead of Yankees. It is patent to all thinking men that

---

[4] Mayes: *History of Education in Mississippi*, p. 282; also "Progress of Education in Mississippi," *Mississippi Teacher*, September, 1889.

[5] Natchez *Democrat*, February 25, 1868.

[6] McNeily: *Provisional Government of Mississippi*, p. 103. Excerpt quoted.

the policy of the South in the new relation with the Negro, is to have him educated to the extent of his capacity and condition. And this should be done by southern people, who will abstain from instilling into the minds of Negroes hatred and distrust of the Southerners. We should be better friends to the Negro than to quietly turn him over to the grasping cupidity of the New Englanders.

The Brandon *Republican* [7] expresses the same opinion and urges southern white teachers to take up the work of instructing Negroes. The Canton *Mail*, in defending a disabled Confederate veteran who was teaching a Negro school at Canton, says:

Who can blame him? He saw, as all sensible men must, that these Negro schools *must* be established throughout our land, and knew too, that it would be much better for southern men to train the minds of young Africa, than to have some red-mouth Radical fill the position.

McNeily quotes the Meridian *Messenger* and the Oxford *Falcon* to almost the same effect. [8] If allowed to go about it in their own way, southern leaders seem to have been perfectly willing to have the Negro educated. Despite the frequent objection to northern teachers, before 1868 the Freedmen's Bureau had numerous applications from planters asking teachers for the freedmen on their plantations, and agreeing to provide suitable schoolhouses on condition that teachers were sent to them. [9] It must be admitted, however, that many of these applications for teachers were prompted by economic rather than by philanthropic motives. Schools were to be established in order to attract labor and to keep the laborers contented.

We must not conclude that there was no opposition to the education of the Negro at any time before 1870, or that there was not a certain element in continuous opposition. The opposition to the Freedmen's Bureau schools was at first more strenuous than it was in any other state. [10] Efforts were made to keep the Bureau agents from finding places to teach; teachers were abused and intimidated. But, by the fall of 1866, if we may accept the word of the Bureau inspector, despite a few 'rabid fire-eaters', a favorable change had taken place in the minds of the people. [11] The excerpts from the

[7] *Provisional Government of Mississippi*, p. 104. Excerpt quoted.
[8] *Ibid.*
[9] Freedmen's Bureau Report, January 1, 1868, p. 33.
[10] *Ibid.*, January 1, 1866.
[11] Freedmen's Bureau Report, January 1, 1867, p. 17.

press previously quoted in this chapter seem to point toward the 'favorable change' referred to by the inspector.

The entry of the Negro into politics in 1868, however, seems to have brought about a reversion of feeling on the part of the Southerners. McNeily claims that General Wood's plan for a system of Negro schools, which had met with such enthusiastic endorsement a year earlier, was never tested out.[12] He adds, "There can be no judgment of its merits, as it was too soon swept away by the surging waves of race distrust and antipathy raised by the ensuing radical policy." The Southerners, later, doubtless not without good reason, viewed with suspicion and alarm the attempt of the Republicans to establish by public taxation a system of free public schools —suspicion and alarm intensified because they were denied the power to say how much they should be taxed to support this system.

In the spring of 1868 the 'Black and Tan Convention', made up largely of carpet-baggers and Negroes, met to draft a constitution. The carpet-baggers were in many cases well-meaning men, able and earnest, but they had slight comprehension of the complex social situation which faced them. That there were many men of doubtful character among them can scarcely be denied. The radical element of the convention soon secured control and proceeded to write into the constitution elaborate provisions for a public school system.

On the floor of the convention the storm center on the question of education hovered about Section 5, [13] which was unanimously reported by the Committee on Public Education, February 3, 1868. This section provided that *a school* should be maintained in *each school district* at least four months in the year, and that no district should receive a share of the school fund if such were not the case. Mr. Stovall, a Republican representative from Carroll County, moved to amend this section by adding:

Provided, That separate schools for the white and colored children be maintained in each district. And provided further, That should there not be a sufficient number of either race to maintain a separate school, the minority race shall have the privilege of sending to school in an adjoining district, and be entitled to their *pro rata* of the school fund the same as if the school was taught in their own district.[14]

[12] McNeily: *Provisional Government of Mississippi*, p. 241.
[13] Journal of Constitutional Convention, 1867–1868, p. 148.
[14] *Ibid.*, p. 316.

The amendment was tabled, as was also a similar provision by Mr. Compton, and a third amendment proposing to subsidize the private schools in sparsely settled districts for the benefit of the minority race.[15] The section on the raising of funds for the establishment and maintenance of the system seems to have passed without much controversy.

There can hardly be any doubt that it was the purpose of the convention to establish a system of 'mixed schools', that is, schools to be attended by the children of both races. This action,[16] combined with the proposition to raise funds for the support of the schools by a property tax, created pronounced opposition on the part of the Southerners to the whole scheme. The *Daily Clarion*, the chief organ of the Democrats in the state, shortly after the tabling of Stovall's amendment, has this to say of the article on education:[17]

As the measure now stands, a fund will be raised by taxing the property of the people to build up a gigantic system of 'Public Education', under the control of imported amalgamationists. The white people, who, it is designated, shall pay this tax, will be admitted to the enjoyment of its benefits only on condition that they will send their children to these mixed schools. This they can never do, without violating all the instincts of their nature, and degrading themselves and polluting their posterity. The scheme practically will amount to their exclusion.

An editorial of a later date indicates the depth of feeling which the suggestion had raised:[18]

No intelligent and true friend of the Negro, much less of the white race, can look upon the measure with any other feeling but of loathing and disgust. In the intent of the authors to set the indestructible laws of God at defiance, and to subvert the usages of the white race in both sections of the Union, they have sown the seeds of ineradicable enmity and discord between the races.

The *Clarion*, however, wished it to be distinctly understood that it did not oppose Negro education, when it denounced in such strenuous language the mixed school proposition.[19]

[15] Journal of Constitutional Convention, 1867–1868, p. 360.
[16] Garner: *Reconstruction in Mississippi*, p. 363.
[17] *Daily Clarion*, February, 1868.
[18] *Ibid.*, February 21, 1868.
[19] *Ibid.*, April 8, 1868.

In concluding this section on the attitude of the southern whites prior to 1870, we may say that it seems clear that the leaders favored the education of the Negro, although many doubted his ability to advance very far. They were ready to coöperate in providing schools for the elevation of the race, asking only a voice in deciding the means for establishing these schools, and in determining the kind of teachers that were to be employed. They were opposed to northern teachers, and endeavored to persuade southern people to become teachers in Negro schools. They felt that northern immigrants did not sympathize with their inbred aversion to social equality with the Negro, and feared that amalgamation of the races would be brought about through mixed schools. Finally, they strenuously objected to being taxed without representation for the support of schools, and more especially did they object at this time because of their sore economic straits. If they had been able to provide the means for the education of the Negro, and had had the assurance that no pernicious doctrines would be instilled into him, it is altogether likely that they would have coöperated heartily in the enterprise.

Attitude of Southern Whites after 1870. The southern white people watched with anxious and suspecting eyes the activities of the carpet-bag government in organizing the new school system. The carpet-bag and Negro elements ratified their constitution in December, 1869. The legislature was forthwith called to draft laws in accordance with its provisions. In the discussion of the Public School Bill, introduced shortly after the session convened, the same questions which had created so much excitement in 1868, namely, the question of mixed schools, and the question of providing the means for maintenance, came to the forefront.

The Public School Bill [20] placed the administration of the schools under a county superintendent, appointed by the state board of education, and under a county board of directors, vested with large powers for the location of schools, for defining the limits of sub-districts, and electing teachers. One section of the bill which caused the Southerners great annoyance read as follows: [21]

Be it enacted, That all children of the state between the ages of five and twenty-one shall have, in all respects, equal advantages in the public schools.

[20] House Journal, 1870, H. B. 352.
[21] Laws of 1870, Chap. I, Sect. 49.

And it shall be the duty of the school directors of any district to establish an additional school in any sub-district thereof, whenever the parents or guardians of twenty-five children of legal school age, and who reside within the limits of the sub-districts, shall make written application to said board for the establishment of the same.

The bill originated in the House, and it was here that the first fight was made upon this objectionable section. Its enemies interpreted this to mean that the school directors might, or might not, establish mixed schools, as they saw fit. Thomas S. Maxey, of Rankin, submitted a minority report [22] of the Educational Committee which had reported favorably upon the bill, declaring that the law should make the establishment of separate schools mandatory, "and thereby give the children of the tax-payers of the state, the benefit of an institution which they are compelled to maintain." In this, Maxey was voicing the opinion of a large majority of the southern white people, not only Democrats but also Republicans. Governor Alcorn, a Republican in politics but a Southerner in sympathy, had previously advised, in a special message,[23] that the legislature "bring to the subject that earnest spirit of justice to both races which demands that the schools be kept absolutely separate."

When the bill reached the Senate the fight was renewed upon the mixed-school feature. On June 28, Lieutenant-Governor R. C. Powers found it necessary to take the floor personally in its defense.[24] His treatment of the subject indicated, at least so far as he was concerned, that the carpet-baggers now had no intention to force white and colored children into the same schools, unless the people so desired it. His point of view may be seen in the following excerpt from his speech:

The provisions of this bill are wise in this respect, for while it recognizes no class distinctions (which of itself should render any law odious in a republican government), it nevertheless consults the convenience and meets all the reasonable demands of the people, by providing for the establishment of an additional school or schools, in any sub-district where the parents or guardians of twenty-five or more children desire it.

This leaves the details of the law where they rightly belong—and where they can be readily arranged, and all conflicting interests harmonized—with

[22] House Journal, 1870, p. 402.
[23] *Ibid.*, Appendix, 1870, pp. 12–20.
[24] Senate Journal, 1870, p. 436.

the people. If the people desire to provide separate schools for white and black, or for good and bad children, or for large and small, or for male and female, there is nothing in this law that prohibits it. The widest latitude is granted, and certainly no class of children in the state can be said to be excluded from school advantages by any provision of the bill.

The lieutenant-governor seems to have been honest in this expression. He failed, however, to take into consideration the depth of prejudice which had been aroused against the government of 'mongrelism', and which made the Southerners suspicious of the political element that had overthrown them. So far as the harmony of the several elements of the Republican party was concerned, his stand was politic, but it would have gone far to allay the suspicion of the southern whites, had he declared himself positively in favor of separate schools. For some time Southerners remained out of sympathy with the school system because they did not know at what time the carpet-baggers might try to force mixed schools upon them.

Not until the Reconstruction officers had begun to perfect the plans for the new system did it dawn upon the Southerners that the mixed school idea had been definitely abandoned. The Hinds County *Gazette* in November, 1870, stated:[25]

We have no idea that the new Board [of Directors of Hinds County] will attempt the great crime of forcing a mixture of the races in the county.

The *Mississippi Educational Journal*, organized as the mouthpiece of the State Department of Education in February of the next year, says:[26]

Since the 'bugbear' of mixed schools for the races which was raised for an evil purpose by the enemies of the system, has been completely demolished, and the purpose of the law and its construction have come to be properly understood, the popular mind has taken hold of the subject with ardent enthusiasm.

Yet, in the discussion of the Civil Rights Bill in Congress, a speech of John R. Lynch [27] (colored) of Mississippi indicates that the mixed school question had not been completely disposed of, even in 1875.

The question which concerned the southern Democrats perhaps even more vitally than the mixed school issue was the question of

[25] Hinds County *Gazette*, November 9, 1870.
[26] *Mississippi Educational Journal*, February, 1870, p. 5.
[27] *Weekly Pilot*, February 20, 1875.

taxation for the support of the schools. Lynch, in his recently published book, *The Facts of Reconstruction*,[28] admits that the storm of protest that went up from the tax-payers when they heard the demands that would be made upon them by the school system, was not without good cause. But he adds, "The Constitution called for the establishment of the system, and of course it had to be done."

As an example of the intensity of feeling upon the subject I will quote, "the most distinguished and widely known school man in the State," Thomas S. Gathright. When, in October, 1870, he was called upon for an expression of opinion on the new school law, he said in part:[29]

> I consider the law referred to, not only a failure in accomplishing good, but an unmitigated outrage upon the rights and liberties of the white people of the state.
>
> I will cite Noxubee County, for an example. The tax to build schoolhouses will be $40,000, and not twenty-five white children in the county can be benefited, while the colored population pay almost no part of this tax. I exhort the friends of our southern children to pay the tax, and then to send their children to their own private schools.

The storm of protest against the obnoxious system of taxation continued well into the next year. It was clearly the chief cause of the 'ku klux' outrages in the eastern counties in 1871. Since tax levies were mainly for the benefit of the schools, the wrath of this mysterious organization was directed against them. Other reasons for the hostility of the order toward the school system have been assigned, but clearly the cause which provoked the outbreak was the expense of the system. Both majority[30] and minority[31] reports of the committee of Congress which investigated these outrages confirm the truth of the above statement.[32]

Hostility to immigrant teachers who were supposed to be teaching the Negroes doctrines of social equality and hatred of southern whites still continued. The reports of the 'ku klux' investigating committee bring out this point. Colonel A. P. Huggins, county superintendent of Monroe County, was beaten and driven from the

[28] Lynch: *The Facts of Reconstruction* (1913), pp. 34, 50, 51.

[29] Hinds County *Gazette*, October 12, 1870.

[30] United States Congress: Report of the Committee on Affairs in the Late Insurrectionary States, p. 75.

[31] *Ibid.*, p. 289.

[32] *cf.*, p. 37.

county because he was the 'instrument' for collecting the taxes, and because the schools which he organized were being taught by foreign teachers suspected of teaching social equality.

Excerpts from contemporary newspapers set forth the southern attitude toward northern teachers. The Hinds County *Gazette* quotes a prominent daily as follows: [33]

> We have it on good authority that the public school teachers imported from the North into several of the counties, are Radical emissaries in disguise, who not only insiduously inculcate the political creed of that party, but are propagandists of its social equality doctrines.

The same paper a month later quotes Horace Greeley's eulogy of the 'Yankee school marm' and makes the following comment: [34]

> The 'school marm' finds her level in the association and the embrace of those that she regards as her equal in every respect. We pity the southern negro, Mr. Greeley, and by no means, the 'school marm'.

The fact that northern white teachers were practically ostracized by the Southerners, and in many places were unable to secure board in white families, probably accounts for their being generally misunderstood by the southern white people.[35] Since they were thus forced to associate to a great extent with Negroes, their motives quite reasonably fell under the suspicion of Southerners unused to such intimacy with the colored race.[36]

I have undertaken thus far in this section to locate the causes for the hostility of the southern people to the public school system. The chief ground for opposition was undoubtedly the expense of establishment and maintenance, an expense to be met by taxation of property owners who had no representation. A second cause for opposition may be found in the fear that mixed schools would be established; and a third, in the character of the teachers that were placed in charge of the schools. We may add finally that there was also opposition, perhaps not so extensive as has been thought, to the education of the Negro.

Northerners seem to have thought that the southern people wished to keep the Negro in ignorance in order to keep him in sub-

[33] Hinds County *Gazette*, March 15, 1871, quotes the *Daily Clarion*.
[34] Mr. Greeley made a visit to Mississippi in 1871 and wrote his impressions in the New York *Tribune*. Hinds County *Gazette*, April 26, 1871.
[35] Garner: *Reconstruction in Mississippi*, p. 359.
[36] Publications, Mississippi Historical Society, vol. xiii, p. 258.

jection.[37] This was doubtless a mistaken judgment since this opinion found expression nowhere in the contemporary southern papers I have examined. Whenever the school system was criticised, usually the education of the Negro was opposed on other grounds previously mentioned.

The fact that southern teachers were frequently advised to teach in Negro schools, and the fact that a number of them did teach in such schools,[38] is evidence that southern people did not so much object to the education of the Negro as they did to the means by which the carpet-baggers were providing it. It was not the public school system that fell under their disfavor, but the abuses which grew out of it.

The Attitude of the Negro toward Education. The Negroes readily listened to the northern immigrants who came among them to teach them how to employ their newly acquired freedom. They seemed to regard the public schools as institutions established for their benefit in particular, and, as long as they were a factor in politics, watched jealously after the interests of the system.[39] The presence among the immigrants of a considerable number of educated Negroes, early pressing forward into the places of leadership in the state, furnished living examples of what education could do. James Lynch, H. R. Revels, and T. W. Cardoza were among the most prominent Negroes in the state, and each of them took a lively interest in education. The *Gazette* (1870–1871) repeatedly referred to the 'school ring' consisting of the state superintendent, the county superintendents, and Lynch, secretary of state and ex-officio member

[37] *Mississippi Educational Journal*, February, 1871, p. 28.

[38] Historians who have covered this era refer to the fact that prominent southern gentlemen and refined southern ladies of good families frequently taught Negro schools. Poverty seems to have driven most of such people to this means of making a livelihood. Garner reports several cases, among which he mentions, a school conducted by the Chancellor of the State University. Superintendent J. H. Alexander of Attala County reported to the State Department in 1872 that several of the "most worthy citizens of the white race were prevailed upon to engage as teachers for this class." The *Mississippi Educational Journal* (1871) pointed with pride to the fact that "in several counties there are ladies employed in colored schools, who a year ago would have thought such employment in the highest sense disgraceful." The 'ku klux' investigating committee called attention to several instances. On the whole, however, the teaching of Negro schools does not seem to have been very general on the part of southern people. The few instances seem to have attracted attention because of their rarity.

[39] Hinds County *Gazette*, October 18, 1876; January 28, 1878; October 26, 1881.

of the Board of Education. Revels was the first Negro to sit in the United States Senate, and later became president of Alcorn University. Cardoza was the second state superintendent. Negro leaders uniformly advocated public education.

The Negroes generally seemed to favor mixed schools as the means of securing equal advantages with the whites. In the Constitutional Convention (1868) they were almost unanimously in favor of tabling the several amendments which proposed the establishment of separate schools.[40] When the mixed school proposition was agitated in the United States Congress in 1875, in connection with the Civil Rights Bill, John R. Lynch, Negro representative from Mississippi, stated the position of the Negroes as follows:[41]

My opinion is that the passage of this bill just as it passed the Senate, will bring mixed schools only in localities where one or the other of the two races is small in numbers, and that in localities where both races are large in numbers, separate institutions of learning will continue to exist, for a number of years at least.

He then went on to say that Negroes did not so much wish to get into the white schools as to make sure that there would be no discrimination against them on account of color. Yet the adoption of his principle would have made mixed schools well nigh universal in the rural districts of Mississippi.

Among the masses of the Negroes, eagerness for education during the Freedmen's Bureau era was at times fairly general, but seemed to decline as they became more and more interested in politics.[42] Night schools numbering seventy-six in 1868 declined to eleven the next year; day schools declined from ninety-eight to seventy, and the enrolment in the schools fell off about a third. Under the Reconstruction régime efforts to secure the passage of a compulsory education law[43] seem to indicate that the masses were not taking advantage of the opportunities furnished them by the school system.

The Attitude of the Northern Whites toward Negro Education. The carpet-baggers, generally speaking, were of the opinion that all that was needed to place the Negro on an equal footing with the

[40] *Daily Clarion*, April 8, 1868.
[41] *Weekly Pilot*, January 20, 1875. (Lynch's speech quoted in full.)
[42] See page 23.
[43] See page 46.

white race, was education. Holding to the Socratic dictum that "knowledge is virtue," they believed that public instruction would cure all the ills of society, physical, mental, and moral. R. C. Powers, one of the most able of their leaders, in his campaign for the lieutenant-governorship in 1869 gave his keynote as follows: [44] "The Negro is a *dangerous element in society because he is ignorant.* Remove the ignorance and there is no more cause for fear."

They were unable to understand the tradition which had bound the southern people to private rather than public education. They had the impression that the southern aristocracy had willfully kept the Negroes and poor whites in ignorance in order to keep the one in slavery, and the other in political subserviency. The *Educational Journal* bears out this statement when it declares that ignorance was responsible for the deplorable condition of the country, as well as the direct cause of the secession:

> The ignorant and illiterate voters throughout the state, and especially where they were in the majority, as in the case of the poorer counties, were the main strength of the secession, and the only class that could be successfully duped into a willful war against the government.[45]

They could not understand the position of the Southerner, who, unused to heavy taxes in the days of his prosperity, raised strenuous objection to a vexatious burden laid upon him by alien hands in the days of his adversity. If the Southerner complained, the carpet-baggers assigned as reasons, hostility to the public school system, and jealousy of the political leverage which the advocacy of popular education had secured for the Republican party.[46]

The northern immigrants were mistaken in believing that they could transplant bodily a northern institution in southern soil and make it grow at once. Their experience in educational affairs had been secured in older and more populous states into which the race question had not entered. The consequence of their error was to array the old southern element solidly against them on the questions of maintenance, mixed schools, foreign teachers, and social doctrines.

In their favor we may say that a large number of them were earnest, conscientious, and animated by high philanthropic motives.

[44] Vicksburg *Daily Times,* October 28, 1869.
[45] *Mississippi Educational Journal,* February, 1871, p. 28.
[46] *Ibid.,* February, 1871, p. 5.

When, at the end of the first year of the organization of the public schools, the machinery was found too expensive, Superintendent Pease [47] was one of the first to advise a change. Governor Powers [48] later advised local officers to be economical and spend less on buildings and furniture. It is hard to believe that the 'Yankee school marms' who faced ostracism from their race in coming to the South, were not of the stuff that martyrs are made of.

[47] House Journal, 1873, p. 729.
[48] Senate Journal, 1873, p. 11.

CHAPTER III

EDUCATIONAL NUCLEUS FORMED BEFORE 1870

In the last chapter we saw that the tax-payers were considerably aroused over the prospect of heavy taxes for the support of the school system. To better comprehend the size of the undertaking, and the amount needed to begin operations, it is necessary to make a hasty survey of the educational situation at that time. Questions which naturally suggest themselves in this connection are: What material equipment was there to begin with? What had been done before 1870 in the way of organizing, grading, and supervising the schools? An attempt to answer these questions will 'be made in the succeeding pages of this chapter.

The Ante-bellum School System. It is not within the scope of this treatise to give a detailed account of the ante-bellum school system, yet a word should be dropped to inform the reader that the state had, prior to 1865, at least recognized the principle of popular education by taking certain very definite steps toward the organization of a system of public schools.[1] When the state came into the Union in 1817, it was provided by an act of Congress that the sixteenth section of every township should be reserved for school purposes. Popular education was further aided by the creation of the Literary Fund in 1821. The sixteenth sections were, by acts of the legislature in 1833 and 1836,[2] turned over to township trustees to be leased to the highest bidders, for a period of ninety-nine years. The trustees were permitted to accept in payment promissory notes on personal security, and, as a consequence of this lax management, most of the sixteenth sections were never paid for. Thus the greater part of the school fund was dissipated before any steps had been taken toward the organization of a school system.

A general school law, passed in March, 1846, proved to be defective, and was later rendered almost useless by privileged local

---

[1] Mayes: *History of Education in Mississippi; The Progress of Education in Mississippi;* chapters on Education in *Memoirs of Mississippi.*

[2] Laws of 1833, p. 452; Laws of 1835.

legislation. Schools were established and received public support, but very little was done toward perfecting the organization of the school system before the Civil War.

The Constitutional Convention of 1865, controlled by native whites, did not modify the article on education which had been written into the constitution of 1832.[3] This was a vague and rather indefinite statement giving the sanction of the state to the principle of popular education. It did not forbid the education of Negroes, yet made no special provision for it.

The legislature, called to meet in the fall of 1865, was too busy defining the political and economic relations of the two races to pay much attention to education. Several acts with reference to the collection or to the investigation of county school funds were passed. These acts, together with an act which modified the apprenticeship law [4] governing the binding out of the children of freedmen, constitute the sum total of the legislation with respect to education. The next legislature, which was also a southern organization, seems to have done nothing worthy of notice.

In this connection we should not fail to take into account the practical training for the actual duties of life which took place upon almost all southern plantations before the Civil War. Planters quite generally selected certain laborers and had them trained in the ordinary trades, such as carpentry, blacksmithing, etc. Then also the conduct of the slaves was regulated to a large extent by the masters. Such training, while not partaking of the character of literary instruction, was no less potent in shaping the life of the ante-bellum Negro.[5]

If anything in the way of material equipment had been provided before 1870 we may be sure it amounted to very little. With respect to this point, John R. Lynch says: [6] "There was not a public school building anywhere in the state except in a few of the larger towns, and they, with possibly a few exceptions, were greatly in

[3] Journal of Constitutional Convention, 1865, Article VIII, Section 14.
[4] The apprenticeship law of 1829 (Laws of 1829, p. 179), governing the binding out of the children of free Negroes, did not require the master to teach the apprentice anything except the 'business or occupation'. The later law (Laws of 1865, Chap. V) did require the master to see that the apprentice was taught to read and write. This seems to represent a fundamental change of attitude in the southern whites.
[5] Weatherford: *Negro Life in the South*, p. 88.
[6] Lynch: *The Facts of Reconstruction*, p. 34.

need of repairs. To erect the necessary school houses and to reconstruct and repair those already in existence so as to afford educational facilities for both races was by no means an easy task."

For the whites, the educational nucleus consisted largely of the ante-bellum academies and private schools which had survived the devastation of war and poverty. The state superintendent in his first report [7] (1871) accounts for 381 private white schools with 391 teachers and 5,249 pupils. At the same time he reports the existence of 53 private colored schools with 49 colored teachers and 1,454 pupils. These latter were largely maintained by northern mission societies and philanthropic organizations.

Activities of the Freedmen's Bureau. In November, 1862, General Grant found it necessary to take some action in order to prevent the large number of Negroes who had attached themselves to his army from seriously embarrassing his commissary.[8] Accordingly, he appointed Chaplain John Eaton as superintendent of Negro affairs in his department, with instructions to "set them to work picking, ginning, and baling all cotton now out and ungathered in the field." Representatives of the various religious and philanthropic organizations followed in the wake of the invading army to assist in the education as well as the relief of the Negroes. The Society of Friends, the American Missionary Association, and the Western Freedmen's Aid Commission were the first in the field.[9] The Freedmen's Department (as it was then called) received orders September 26, 1863, to aid these representatives with transportation, rations, and places in which to teach. Beyond giving advice in regard to the distribution of teachers and the location of schools, the superintendent of the department exercised no control over their activities. Complications soon arose among the societies. Some central authority was necessary to insure regularity of tuition fees, and uniformity in other matters of administration.[10] General Eaton, September 26, 1864, was authorized to designate certain officers as superintendents of colored schools, and the department assumed general supervision of the educational work.

[7] Report of Superintendent, 1871, Statistics.
[8] P. S. Pierce: *The Freedmen's Bureau*, p. 9. Grant's claim to having first initiated work for the freedmen does injustice to the claims of Generals Butler, Wool, and Sherman, who worked independently about the same time.
[9] Eaton: *Grant, Lincoln and the Freedmen*, Chap. XIV.
[10] *Ibid.*

An act of Congress, July 16, 1866, enlarged the powers of the Bureau for educational purposes. The work heretofore accomplished had been done without the authorization of Congress.[11] Funds for teachers, books, and the furnishing of buildings had been derived from the rent of abandoned property. This act also authorized coöperation with private benevolent societies. An appropriation of $500,000 in 1867, and still another appropriation in 1868, materially aided the work of the Bureau.

The Bureau did extensive work in Mississippi until 1870. The work was at first conducted under the supervision of Rev. Joseph Warren, and after his removal in the latter part of 1866,[12] it was carried on by Captain H. R. Pease, who later became state superintendent.[13] An idea of the scope and progress of the undertaking may be had by an examination of the statistical summary here given.

There was at first "inveterate opposition" to the work of the Bureau on the part of the southern white people. This opposition manifested itself in threatening teachers and in preventing the agents of the Bureau from securing places to teach. It had disappeared to a large extent by the spring of 1867, but the report of the inspector, January 1, 1868, seems to indicate that opposition had revived. In one section this turn of public sentiment was attributed to the "recent so-called radical reaction in the North." [14] The political situation in the state was no doubt in large measure responsible for the change.

At first the Negroes showed the "usual eagerness to learn," but attendance in the schools seems throughout the whole period to have been very irregular. Cotton picking probably interfered with the attendance in the fall. The excitement of the triumphant entry of the Negro element into state politics caused a decided slump in the attendance in 1869 and 1870.[15] A constant falling off in the number of night schools established for adults, indicates that the interest of the Negroes had waned considerably. General Superintendent Alvord in 1868 estimated that one colored child of school

[11] P. S. Pierce: *The Freedmen's Bureau*, p. 76.
[12] Inspector's Report, January 1, 1867, p. 17.
[13] *Ibid.*, June 30, 1867, p. 33.
[14] *Ibid.*, January 1, 1868, p. 34.
[15] *Ibid.*, January 1, 1870, p. 35.

age out of every fifteen was enrolled in the schools.[16] This was the lowest ratio of all southern states.

The organization of Sunday schools was first begun by southern citizens in the spring of 1866.[17] The nature of the instruction offered in freedmen's schools appears not to have produced the moral results which had been expected by the Bureau.[18] An effort was made to remedy this situation in 1868 by the organization of

TABULAR VIEW OF THE ACTIVITIES OF THE FREEDMEN'S
BUREAU IN MISSISSIPPI, 1866–1870

(Compiled from the Semi-Annual Reports of the Inspector)

	1866		1867		1868		1869		1870
	January	July	January	July	January	July	January	July	January
Night schools				20	76	29	13	11	16
Day schools				46	56	98	79	70	56
Both	34	50	42	66	132	127	92	81	72
White teachers				73		83	60	65	61
Colored teachers				9		45	40	40	29
Both		80		82		128	100	105	90
Enrolment		5,407	2,129	4,697		6,253	4,003	4,344	3,475
Average attendance				3,549			3,062	3,361	2,586
Sabbath schools			21						45
White pupils						51	24	47	7

temperance societies; thirty societies were organized that year. The laxness of the domestic relations of the sexes was another problem which vexed the Bureau. On the subject of looseness of morals, Superintendent Pease had this to say in 1869:[19] "There has not been the advancement in the moral condition of the freed people, commensurate with their education and general intelligence." Accordingly, he began to wage a campaign for temperance and purity, making addresses in various parts of the state. He also took pains to discipline immoral teachers.

[16] Inspector's Report, January 1, 1868, p. 47.
[17] *Ibid.*, July 1, 1866, p. 7.
[18] *Ibid.*, January 1, 1869, p. 29.
[19] *Ibid.*, January 1, 1869, p. 29.

The Bureau officials, particularly in the early days of the organization, manifested great confidence in the ability of letters and book-learning to function in the lives of the Negroes.[20] After a year or two of experience, however, they came to acknowledge the importance of training, both manual and moral, and to emphasize—at least in theory—this form of education.

Instruction in the early days was of course very elementary. "Education for the freedmen," says the first semi-annual Report of the Inspector,[21] "as a whole, must be at first very rudimentary, in which the text will be found mainly in the spelling book, but which can become, as soon as possible, universal." In the second Report [22] we find a similar statement: "With the Bible, spelling-book, and freedom as the basis of instruction, the poorest teaching is better than the present ignorance."

Day schools were organized for children, and night schools for adults, but we have no evidence that children received one form of instruction and adults another. In 1868, there were 2,710 pupils studying "spelling and easy reading." Needle-work, introduced in 1868, appears to have been the only form of manual work taught in the schools, and even this does not seem to have been very popular. The highest enrolment in this subject was reached in 1869 when 154 pupils were being trained, but during the next year the number dropped to thirty-four.

Two aims of education were formulated in 1869 by the Bureau:[23]

First. Moral culture should be paramount in our plans; the conscious practical aim in all our schools . . .

Second. The various affairs and economies of everyday life should be taught; cleanliness, dress, home habits, social proprieties, uses of furniture, preparation of food, and tasteful construction of buildings, though with rustic materials; also industry, and individual self-reliance; labor productive of support and thrift; habits of saving, with the right use of what is saved.

It was further suggested that industrial science and art be brought into the higher schools, and that music and temperance be taught. The activities of the Bureau were discontinued before any attempt was made to put these theories into practice. Here, how-

---

[20] Inspector's Report, January 1, 1866, p. 1.
[21] *Ibid.*, p. 12.
[22] *Ibid.*, July 1, 1866.
[23] *Ibid.*, July 1, 1869.

ever, were laid down the principles which have been worked out in such schools as Hampton, Tuskegee, and Tougaloo.

There were several contributions which the Freedmen's Bureau made to Negro education in Mississippi.

First, the schools served to awaken the Negroes to the need of education.

Second, they gave rudimentary instruction to a considerable number of Negroes, thus partially fitting them to become teachers in the public schools. The Freedmen's Bureau pupils were beginning to teach in 1869.[24]

Third, the Bureau prepared the ground for the organization of the public school system. The state had been divided into twenty-one sub-districts [25] and an effort had been made to establish schools in every part of the state, so there were doubtless few, if any, places so remote that the Negroes had not heard of the advantages to be derived from education.

Fourth, the Bureau provided a centralized scheme of organization which could easily be taken over by the state authorities. Mr. Pease in 1870 said: "In all the principal cities and towns the schools are thoroughly classified, graded, and conducted by earnest, thorough and practical teachers." [26] The experience which this gentleman had gained from managing the affairs of the Bureau made him possibly the best man that the Republicans could have selected to inaugurate the new school system. When he assumed the duties of state superintendent, he still retained his position with the Bureau.[27]

Fifth, the Bureau left material equipment in the form of buildings and furniture which could be utilized. While there are only twelve school buildings reported as owned by freedmen in 1870, a considerable number of rented buildings had been furnished by the Bureau.

The Peabody Fund. The Peabody Fund was created in February, 1867, for the benefit of the cause of education in the southern states. The first distribution of the fund was made in 1868. Nine towns and one private institute were aided with small amounts this year.[28]

---

[24] Inspector's Report, July 1, 1869, p. 44.
[25] *Ibid.*, July 1, 1868, p. 34.
[26] *Ibid.*, January 1, 1870, p. 35.
[27] *Ibid.*, p. 29.
[28] Proceedings, Peabody Fund, 1868, p. 108.

So far as can be determined, the donations to these towns were for the benefit of white schools. In 1869, on account of the uncertain political situation in the state, only six towns were aided.

In the Peabody report for 1868, it is interesting to note that there were 3,000 children of school age in the city of Vicksburg, one-half of whom were colored, and that there were 1,130 colored children in school. The town was given two thousand dollars on condition that it enlarge its corps of teachers so as to "admit all white children that apply."[29] The Negro pupils here referred to were doubtless in Freedmen's Bureau schools.

From the information which we have at hand it appears that the public school system had to be built from the ground up. Not only did buildings have to be erected, but a working organization had to be provided, and teachers had to be imported to meet the demands made for properly qualified instructors in both white and colored schools. Such was the situation that faced the Reconstruction government in the spring of 1870.

[29] Proceedings, Peabody Fund, 1868, p. 108.

CHAPTER IV

EDUCATION DURING THE RECONSTRUCTION

The Organization of the System. The constitution of 1869 was drafted by the famous 'Black and Tan Convention', dominated by the carpet-bag and Negro elements. In this convention the former slave holders formed a hopeless minority. On February 3, 1868, the Committee on Public Education made a unanimous report on the provision for education, which, with a few minor amendments, was adopted almost as proposed.[1]

The legislature was authorized to establish a uniform system of free public schools for the benefit of all children between the ages of five and twenty-one, and to establish schools of higher grade as soon as practicable.[2] The system was placed under the supervision of a state superintendent,[3] to be elected by the people at the same time and in the same manner as the governor, for a four-year term. There was also to be a state board of education,[4] consisting of the state superintendent, the secretary of state, and the attorney general, vested with the management of the school funds and with such other authority as should be prescribed by law. The state superintendent was empowered to appoint county superintendents for two-year terms.[5] He was further authorized to report to the legislature within twenty days after its first session, a uniform system of free public schools.[6]

A school fund was provided [7] by the setting aside of the following: (1) Funds derived from swamp lands granted to the state for school purposes (with certain exceptions); (2) funds derived from the lands vested in the state by escheat, purchase, or forfeiture for taxes; (3) fines collected for the breach of penal laws, and all

[1] Journal of Constitutional Convention, 1865, p. 148.
[2] Constitution of 1869, Article VIII, Section 1.
[3] *Ibid.*, Section 2.
[4] *Ibid.*, Section 3.
[5] *Ibid.*, Section 4.
[6] *Ibid.*, Section 5.
[7] *Ibid.*, Section 6.

moneys received for licenses granted for the sale of intoxicating liquors; (4) all moneys paid as an equivalent for exemption from military duty, funds arising from the consolidation of the township funds, and moneys donated to the state for school purposes. The school fund was to be invested in United States bonds. It might be increased but not diminished. The interest was to be inviolably appropriated to the public schools. A poll tax of two dollars for school purposes was made permissive. The fund was to be disbursed to the counties on the basis of the number of children of school age.

During the debate on the article on education, two provisions were made the points of attack. The first was the section allowing the state superintendent to appoint the county superintendents.[8] After a spirited debate, it was decided to make the office appointive, but to empower the legislature to make it elective. The storm center, however, hovered about the question whether or not the constitution should make one set of schools accommodate both races. From the nature of the discussion, which has been given elsewhere in this treatise, it is clear that the framers of the constitution favored mixed schools. When they said, "A school shall be maintained in each school district at least four months in the year . . ."[9] they certainly regarded the district as the smallest unit of organization, and possibly only the shrewdest of their number anticipated the later definition of the term as a county comprehending a number of sub-districts.

Other sections of the article on education were accepted by the members of the convention with little discussion. The sections chiefly objected to by the southern press were Section 5, relating to mixed schools, and Section 10, which empowered the legislature to levy and collect such taxes as were needed to maintain the school system. The constitution, drafted by this convention was ratified by the electorate, that is, by the Negro and carpet-bag element, December 1, 1869.

In the spring of 1870, the officers elected under the new constitution took their seats. Honorable J. L. Alcorn, a southern leader who had turned Republican under the persuasion that the best interests of the state would be subserved by pursuing a policy

[8] Constitution of 1869, Article VIII, Section 4.
[9] *Ibid.*, Section 5.

of conciliation, was installed as governor. In his inaugural address he declared himself strongly in favor of the establishment of a system of common schools for the benefit of the "poor white and colored children of the state who had been permitted in the past to grow up like wild flowers." A special message on education,[10] shortly after his installation, outlined a plan for the organization of the school system. First, he asserted that the most imperative need of the state was that of trained teachers. To provide for this need he recommended the appropriation of $20,000 for the purchase of Tougaloo University, a Negro school belonging to the American Missionary Association, to be used for a state normal and agricultural school for the colored race. He believed that there should be a normal school for each race but that the colored normal was most urgent at this time. The governor's plan for the organization of the system was derived from a study of the New York and Pennsylvania systems. Two points for which he stood emphatically were separate schools for the races, and local election or appointment of county superintendents. On these points the legislature differed with him. In regard to the launching of the system, he favored a gradual up-building which would not tax too heavily the impoverished tax-payers.

As we have seen, the constitution had erected the framework about which the system was to be built when it had provided for a state school fund, had established the state board of education, had created the elective office of state superintendent, and had decreed that county superintendents should be appointed by the state department unless other provision were made. The legal status of the system was further defined by the legislature on July 4, 1870.

At the head of the system was the state board of education [11] with general supervision over all school funds, empowered to appoint county superintendents with the confirmation of the Senate, and to remove these officers for incompetency or neglect of duty. The state superintendent [12] was made the chief administrative officer. He was given general supervision of the system, required to prescribe rules for organization, decide disputes, solicit reports from

---

[10] House Journal, Appendix, pp. 12–20.
[11] Laws of 1870, Chap. I, Sections 1, 12, 13.
[12] *Ibid.*, Section 14.

state institutions, visit schools, and provide for the holding of teachers' institutes in each congressional district.

The county was made the unit of local organization.[13] A board of six school directors,[14] appointed by the county board of supervisors to represent the several supervisors' districts, were delegated with the functions of local administration. The directors were appointed for a three-year period of service, their terms expiring at different times. They were to receive mileage and a *per diem* of three dollars for actual service. They were vested with corporate powers, and also empowered to form sub-districts, to fix the boundaries of these to suit the convenience of the people, to purchase grounds and erect buildings, to establish union or graded schools wherever necessary, to prescribe texts, to hire teachers, and to furnish the board of supervisors with an estimate of the cost of school sites, construction and rental of buildings, repairs, fuel, etc.

The county superintendent [15] was the administrative officer of the school district. Besides being given general supervision of the schools of the county, he was required to examine and certificate teachers, to report to the state department annually on the condition of the schools, school lands, etc., to report to the state auditor the enumeration of the educable children, and to perform such other duties as should be specified by the state department. He was to receive a *per diem* of five dollars for actual service.

The system of education was to be established and maintained largely by local taxation. It is true that a state school fund had been provided for by the constitution, but since the amount of available funds embraced by this was small, a tax was necessary to furnish the means for equipping and supporting the schools. The boards of directors were authorized by law to furnish the county boards of supervisors with an estimate [16] of the funds needed to run the schools of the district, and the supervisors were required to levy a tax on the property of the county to meet this expense. Taxes thus

[13] Laws of 1870, Chap. I, Section 2.

[14] In towns of 5,000 and over, the boards of aldermen appointed the directors of the separate district, selecting representatives, as far as possible, from the several wards. Such boards were given the same powers as county directors. Since, however, there were less than half a dozen towns of this class, at this time, we need not consider the separate district in this connection (Section 23).

[15] Laws of 1870, Chap. I, Section 19.

[16] *Ibid.*, Sections 27, 32.

levied were to be kept separate from the state apportionment. It was provided also that there should be separate levies for a schoolhouse fund and for a teachers' fund. The maximum levy for the schoolhouse fund was fixed at ten mills, and the maximum levy for the teachers' fund at five mills.

The Operation of the System. I. The public school system, legally organized in July, 1870, went into operation in the fall of that year under the leadership of State Superintendent H. R. Pease.[17] The law required that county superintendents should be appointed by the state department, and that the county school directors should be appointed by the county boards of supervisors. As no election of county and local officers [18] was held until November, 1871, the duty of appointing the county supervisors devolved upon the military governor, General Ames. The appointees were in most cases Republicans, 'scalawags', if not Negroes and carpet-baggers. Thus, the local units were permitted to take no hand in the initiation of the system. The loss of the right to determine the personnel of the boards of directors was of graver consequence than the loss of the right to elect the county superintendents. The directors had the power of establishing schools, fixing the boundaries of sub-districts, erecting and equipping buildings, and fixing the amount of the tax levy. The southern whites, who constituted the tax-payers, were given no voice in determining how much they should be taxed.

There was good reason for a highly centralized organization for the installation of the system. Centralization insured the establishment of schools in all counties; it provided for a sufficient tax levy to maintain the schools; it saw that the Negroes were not overlooked. On the other hand, it vested the power of raising local funds in the hands of men who were not required to share the burdens which they imposed; who, in many cases, had lived only a short time in the state, and consequently had little appreciation of the difficulty the southern whites were having in trying to adjust themselves to the new economic situation; who often belonged to the less worthy class of immigrants, with no experience in the

---

[17] Henry R. Pease, a native of Connecticut, a Federal captain, and later agent of the Freedmen's Bureau. It devolved upon him to organize the public school system. His competency has never been questioned. He stepped from the state superintendency into the United States Senate. Rowland's *Mississippi.*

[18] Garner: *Reconstruction in Mississippi,* p. 357.

affairs of government, and with the selfish exploitation of the country too often as their only excuse for being there. The evils bred by this plan of organization were legion. Misunderstandings arose where none should have existed; injustice was done when none was intended; lack of sympathy was at first well nigh universal; fraud and corruption were not infrequent.

The expense of establishing schools, even under ordinary circumstances, falls heavily upon the tax-payers. Under the demoralized economic circumstances of the period, it was felt with crushing effect. The machinery had been borrowed from older, richer, and more populous states, and was consequently too expensive for Mississippi. The six county directors drew a *per diem* of three dollars, and mileage at ten cents a mile; the circuit clerk drew a *per diem* of three dollars for acting as secretary of the board of directors; the superintendent drew a *per diem* of five dollars; and the boards of supervisors, to whom the directors had to report their estimate of the levy for schools, drew six dollars and mileage for each of their six members. This complicated machinery was not only expensive but unnecessary. It cost the state during the second year, $100,000, of which the state superintendent says $50,000 was "absolutely thrown away." [19]

Superintendent Pease recognized [20] at the close of the first year that the cost of the schools was far exceeding his expectations. The chief fault was with the machinery for local administration. "The experience of the last twelve months," says he, "shows that notwithstanding we have succeeded in establishing a large number of schools, the work has been accomplished at the expense of an enormous and unnecessary outlay of labor and money." The zeal of the local officers in founding schools, in building school houses, and in levying taxes for maintenance, carried them to an extreme which staggered even the Reconstruction leaders. Governor Powers in 1873 urged [21] that the school funds be spent mainly for teachers, and that less be spent on "costly houses, expensive boards of managers, and elaborate outfits."

[19] House Journal, 1873, p. 729.
[20] Superintendent's Report, 1871, p. 16.
[21] Senate Journal, 1873, p. 11.

The following figures from the report of the state superintendent[22] will give an idea of the accomplishment and cost of the first year's work:

Schoolhouses built for whites	230
Schoolhouses built for Negroes	252
Sites purchased	128
Sites donated	177
Cost of school sites	$33,921
Cost of school buildings	157,374
Rent of schoolhouses	25,601
Contingent expenses, fuel, etc.	20,731
School furniture	34,861
Apparatus	5,406
School books	14,481
Average monthly salary of teachers	58.90
Salaries of county superintendents	35,072
Total salaries of teachers	624,233
Total cost of boards of directors	58,000

The number of schools put into operation the first year was 3,450, and the value of school property was estimated at $800,000.[23] The number of sites that were purchased cost on the average about $265; and the houses erected on these sites cost on the average $325. The number of buildings erected for Negroes was slightly more than the number erected for whites. Expenditures, as a whole, were not excessive as figures run to-day, but considering the impoverished condition of the country at that time, they fell rather heavily.

As we have seen, schoolhouses had to be built and furnished and teachers had to be paid from the local revenue. It is true that there was a state school fund of $1,950,000, but it existed only in name, and the schools received no benefit from it.[24] The raising of the state tax levy from one mill in 1869 to five mills in 1870, while not for the benefit of the schools, increased the sum total of the taxes, and tended to augment discontent with the whole system of taxation. To make matters worse, a law was passed which changed

[22] Superintendent's Report, 1871, Statistics.
[23] This estimate is probably excessive.
[24] Superintendent's Report, 1871.

the date for the collection of taxes. The levy for the past year, due in April, was suspended till July. The new levy was made to fall due in December.[25] This made two levies fall due within six months. And to cap the climax, the cotton crop of 1870 was a failure, and there was nothing with which to pay.

The expense of establishing Negro schools was heavy. Although the Freedmen's Bureau had left a slight equipment, it was by no means adequate. The log cabin had been considered good enough for the Negro's home and church before the war, but the northern enthusiasts were now insisting that frame school buildings be constructed and equipped with patented desks and other modern furnishings. The *Gazette* complains [26] of the lavish expenditures for "fine walnut desks, cane seat chairs, elegant settles," etc., and adds this interesting datum: "In all the history of this community the school children have supplied each for himself his own desk, chair, etc., and they have been of such styles as could be furnished from the household goods. The white schools of the town [Raymond] and vicinity are thus furnished now." The southern whites generally viewed the purchase of fine furniture with suspicion and alarm.[27]

Cause for additional expense was provided in the fact that there were no colored teachers. For the 860 schools for Negroes in 1871 there were 400 Negro teachers. White teachers had to be secured for over half of these schools. Southern whites did not take to the profession in numbers sufficient to man the Negro schools.[28] Hence, northern teachers had to be imported, and since a term of four months with low salaries would not furnish remuneration sufficient to attract this class of teachers, the monthly salaries had to be raised. The average monthly salary for 1871 was $58.90. There is no record that teachers of Negro schools for this period received less than teachers of white schools.

The local officials had little sympathy with the tax-payer struggling with the new economic situation. They launched at once upon the installation of the school system with little regard to costs. It is estimated that the cost of the schools of Chickasaw County for 1871, if the Reconstructionists had been permitted to

[25] United States Congress: Report of Committee on Affairs in Southern States, p. 373.
[26] Hinds County *Gazette*, February 1, 1871.
[27] United States Congress: Report of Committee on Affairs in Southern States, 1872.
[28] See page 16.

carry out their program, would have amounted to $120,000 for teachers and $100,000 for schoolhouses.[29] In Lowndes County, where the Negro children outnumbered the white children four to one, sixty public schools were opened and teachers were employed at salaries ranging from $50 to $150 per month, the average being $78.[30] A special tax of $95,000 was levied by the supervisors, but upon protest this was cut to half the amount. These examples are typical.

It is quite natural that charges of fraud and corruption would be brought by the tax-payers, since they had no hand in making the levies. In many cases these charges were well founded. Mr. James Sykes, a prominent citizen of Lowndes County, testified [31] before the 'ku klux' investigating committee that a tax of $3,800 was levied upon the sub-district in which he lived, to support two schools. Upon investigation, he found that the county had been charged with $360 for rent, fuel, and repairs on an old church which he had built for his Negroes before the war, and for which no rent had been charged, and no repairs made. In Washington County, J. P. Ball, a mulatto photographer from Cincinnati, was chairman of the board of supervisors, and his son was clerk of the school board.[32] Young Ball was in 1873 voted $1,700 for stationery. Seven hundred dollars was voted for a schoolhouse at Leota which was never erected. McNeily, whose article in the Publications of the Mississippi Historical Society is in part a primary source, states: "All over the state the robbery through the school system was especially rank." In 1871, the Brandon *Republican* [33] declared, "The manner in which the School Boards of some counties are swindling the people, is enough to drive them mad . . ."

The arbitrary demands of the Reconstructionists were no sooner felt than there sprang up violent opposition to the school system. In the eastern counties of the state this opposition found expression in 'ku klux' raids in which schoolhouses were burned and obnoxious teachers driven from the country. Both majority and minority reports of the committee of Congress which investigated these out-

[29] United States Congress: Report of Committee on Affairs in Southern States, 1872, p. 377.

[30] *Ibid.*, 1872, Minority Report.

[31] *Ibid.*, 1872.

[32] Publications of Mississippi Historical Society, Vol. IX, p. 150.

[33] Hinds County *Gazette*, March 22, 1871, quoted.

rages, while differing in point of view, gave as the unmistakable cause of the trouble, hostility to the school system. This hostility was, in the main, due to the excessive tax levies which had been laid upon the people. The majority report emphasized also the fact that there was "hostility to all free schools, and especially to free schools for colored children."[34] Both intimate that there was opposition to colored schools and northern emissaries.

Upon reading the reports of the 'ku klux' investigating committee, one is forced to the conclusion that no one of the causes mentioned, except that of the heavy tax levy, was sufficient to provoke an outbreak. This is perfectly clear in the testimony of the two chief witnesses, Colonel H. P. Huggins and Charles Baskerville. Opposition to the schools on the ground that they were instructing Negroes and instilling in them doctrines of social equality, is given as a clearly incidental cause. Garner makes[35] the pertinent observation that since both white and colored schools were burned and closed, and since both ex-Union and ex-Confederate teachers were victims, opposition was directed not against the public school system *per se*, but against its abuses.

The 'ku klux' outrages seem to have been confined to the eastern counties of the state, so far as they affected the school system in 1870–1871. Superintendent Huggins of Monroe County was whipped, chiefly on the charge that he was the 'instrument' for collecting the taxes. Two school directors of the same county, who had voted to levy the tax, were warned to resign, and did so. The teachers of twenty-six schools on the east side of the Tombigbee River were similarly forced to close their schools. Cornelius McBride, teacher of a Negro school in Chickasaw County, was whipped on the charge that he was teaching one of the expensive schools maintained by the Radicals. All the schoolhouses in Winston County were burned in March, 1871, and all the churches in which Negro schools were being maintained.[36] Outrages were reported from Monroe, Noxubee, Chickasaw, Winston, and Pontotoc Counties.

There were doubtless outrages in other parts of the state, but they cannot be definitely traced to the 'ku klux'. For instance, three colored schoolhouses in Hinds County were burned in the

[34] United States Congress: Report of Committee on Affairs in Southern States, p. 73.
[35] Garner: *Reconstruction in Mississippi*, p. 360.
[36] *Mississippi Educational Journal*, March, 1871, p. 131.

spring of 1871, but it is not recorded that the 'ku klux' had anything to do with the burning.[37]

The chief ground for opposition to the school system was not the education of the Negro, as many people think, but the cost of maintaining an expensive system at a time when the southern people were least able to support it. This fact, combined with the fact that the tax-payers were deprived of the right to say what expenditures should be made, caused widespread discontent. The Hinds County *Gazette* (1870–1871) repeatedly referred to the 'school ring', composed of Lynch, Pease, and the county superintendents, as an organization to defraud the people. This paper declared itself in favor of universal education and popular taxation, but strenuously objected to the abuses of the administration under the Reconstructionists.[38]

A forecast of this form of opposition may be found in a joint protest of six state senators against the Public School Bill in 1870. This protest was directed against a system of taxation so burdensome "as to excite in their [the people's] minds a strong prejudice against the establishment of public schools."[39] Mayes says that the school system was regarded as a system of taxation without representation, "imposed by adventurers and plunderers rather for the purpose of riveting their fetters on the people of the state, than for any humanitarian purpose."[40]

We must, however, credit some of the state officers of the Reconstruction period with honest intentions. Alcorn [41] was from the first opposed to an expensive outlay for schools; Pease [42] discovered the error in the organization of the local machinery at the close of the first year, and got a bill to remedy the situation reported favorably in the House in 1871; Powers,[43] when he became governor in 1873, advised against heavy taxation for buildings and furniture. The fault seems to have lain largely with the local administration.

---

[37] *Mississippi Educational Journal*, p. 88.
[38] Hinds County *Gazette*, February 22, 1871.
[39] Senate Journal, 1870, p. 445.
[40] *Memoirs of Mississippi*, Vol. II, p. 338 (Goodspeed's edition).
[41] House Journal, Appendix, 1870, pp. 12–20; *Mississippi Educational Journal*, March, 1871.
[42] House Journal, 1873, p. 715.
[43] Senate Journal, 1873, p. 11.

II. A vigorous campaign for the establishment of schools was launched by State Superintendent Pease and his co-laborers as soon as the school bill was approved in July, 1870. The state superintendent was undoubtedly a capable and energetic worker. The schools established were classified as primary, grammar, high, and mixed-grade schools. (See Table I) The mixed-grade school was the institution that best served the needs of the rural commu-

TABLE I

ENROLMENT AND ATTENDANCE IN WHITE AND COLORED
SCHOOLS, 1870–1871

(*Compiled from Report of State Superintendent, 1871*)

	WHITE		COLORED	
	Schools	*Enrolment*	*Schools*	*Enrolment*
Primary schools	535	18,312	603	26,303
Grammar schools	400	14,423	51	2,641
High schools	78	5,045	4	640
Mixed grade schools	729	24,577	202	12,370
Total	1,739[44]	66,257[44]	860[44]	45,429[44]

nities; the primary school was practically all that was needed for Negroes at this stage of their educational progress. Only four high schools were established for Negroes, and only a third as many mixed-grade colored schools as primary. No effort to mingle the races in the schools seems to have been made. Only two mixed schools were reported this year, or ever after.

It will be observed from a study of Table II that the number of educable colored children in 1871 outnumbered the educable whites nearly 7,000. The white schools enrolled a larger proportion than did the colored, but the average daily attendance of the Negroes was greater than that of the whites.

[44] The author is not responsible for errors in the computing of totals. The corrected totals for the above are: White schools, 1,742; enrolment, 62,357. Colored enrolment, 41,954.

By 1872 the opposition to public schools had to some extent simmered down. Superintendent Pease reported to the United States Commissioner in this year that public sentiment had undergone a "most marvelous revolution."[45] The 'ku klux' activities of the previous year died out completely. There were still a few who opposed the general principle of taxation for public schools. These "fossil

TABLE II

SCHOOL POPULATION, ENROLMENT, AND AVERAGE
ATTENDANCE, 1870–1871

(*Compiled from Report of State Superintendent, 1870–1871*)

	White	Colored
Children, five to twenty-one years	120,073	126,769
Enrolled in schools	66,257	45,429
Per cent. of children enrolled	55.2[46]	35.9[46]
Average attendance	45,290	36,040
Per cent. of those enrolled in average attendance	74.4[46]	79.3[46]

theorists," as Mr. Pease called them, objected especially to paying taxes for the support of Negro schools.[47]

As for the Negroes, they were heartily in favor of heavy taxes for schools. The Superintendent argued that they, as the industrial class, received indirectly the burden of taxation, and consequently should have the deciding voice in determining what tax, and how much, should be levied. It is needless to say that there were few, if any southern tax-payers, who could follow this line of reasoning.

If the voices of criticism raised against the school system had subsided as much as the state superintendent says they had, we may imagine that the silence was, to say the least, grim. The financial condition of the state had gone from bad to worse. Mis-

---

[45] Computed by the author.
[46] United States Commissioner's Report, 1872, p. 197.
[47] *Ibid.*, 1873, p. 213.

management and extravagance in the Reconstruction government continued until the state was on the verge of bankruptcy long before 1875. In two years, from 1870 to 1872, the indebtedness of the state more than doubled.[48] Lack of credit abroad began at once to be felt. State funds were invested in state warrants which were forced upon the people as the medium of circulation. Speculation in these by state officials caused them rapidly to depreciate in value.[49] The assessed valuation of real property decreased from $118,000,000 in 1870 to $109,000,000 in 1874; personal property decreased in value from $59,000,000 to $47,000,000 during the same period. By 1876, real property had fallen to $95,097,450, and personal property to $35,000,000.[50]

The perilous condition of the finances of the state was repeatedly pointed out, but the policy of extravagance was continued. Heavy taxes were levied to meet the heavy expenditures of the state's governmental machinery. The state tax levy rose from one mill in 1869 to fourteen mills in 1874.[51] County tax levies were piled upon this. In one county in 1874 the total tax levy amounted to twenty-three and two-tenths mills. Such levies were confiscatory. This astounding statement comes from the auditor of public accounts in 1874:[52]

The state now holds not less than 4,500,000 acres of land forfeited for taxes. In addition to this, the several Levee Boards in the Levee Districts, hold 1,500,000 acres more, on which the state tax was suspended. This makes an aggregate of 6,000,000 acres, or one-fifth of the entire area of the state.

The school fund suffered in common with other state funds. During the five years from 1870 to 1874, there were placed to the credit of the school fund $1,057,929, and disbursed only $342,052.[53] This should have left a balance to the credit of the fund of $715,877. According to the constitution, this money should have been invested in United States bonds, but instead, it had been invested in state warrants which had been cancelled.[54] From this large sum, only

[48] Report of State Treasurer, 1872, p. 4.
[49] *Ibid.*, 1873, p. 5.
[50] State Auditor's Report, 1876, p. v.
[51] Garner: *Reconstruction in Mississippi*, p. 323, (table).
[52] Auditor of Public Accounts, 1874, p. 7.
[53] Report of State Treasurer, 1874, Statement E.
[54] Auditor of Public Accounts, 1874, p. 6.

$66,617 was invested as had been directed. When the southern people again took charge of the government there was left in the treasury to the credit of the school fund a balance of $60,920.21. This amount was increased by the addition of $104,009.60 from fines, forfeitures, and licenses, permitted by the laws of 1876, making a total of $164,935.87, or fifty-two cents for each educable child.[55] These figures are sufficient to indicate the deplorable condition of school funds during the Reconstruction era.

The expensive program of organization, begun in 1871, was carried on more extravagantly the next year. The following table, compiled from the reports of the state superintendent for these years, gives an idea of the cost of organization.

	1871	*1872*	*1874*
Buildings and repairs	$157,347	$176,917	$35,059
Mileage and *per diem* of directors	58,000(est.)	70,000	
Salaries of county superintendents	35,072		46,000
Total cost of county officers	93,072 [56]	145,000	
Total salaries of teachers	624,233	584,536	737,548
Average monthly salaries of teachers	58.90	51.32	
Total costs	950,000	976,553	842,603

During the second year 432 additional schoolhouses were built; the total number of schools increased from 3,450 to 4,650 (thirty-five per cent.), and the number of teachers increased from 3,193 to 4,800 (fifty per cent.). As is evident from the figures in the table, the boards of directors furnished one of the heaviest items of expense. The complaints of the tax-payers were both loud and deep. The governor and the state superintendent exerted themselves to find a remedy for the situation.[57]

The local machinery, in addition to being expensive, was far from harmonious. The duties of the directors conflicted with those of the county superintendent.[58] "Efforts to avoid too much centralization

[55] Auditor of Public Accounts, 1876, p. v.
[56] Computed from second and third items above.
[57] The superintendent had had his measure reported favorably by the House Committee on Education in 1872. See also Message of Governor Powers, January 21, 1873.
[58] United States Commissioner's Report, 1873, p. 213.

resulted in the opposite extreme." Superintendent Pease declared that a sweeping reorganization of the system was necessary in order to make it fit the conditions of the time. At the meeting of the legislature in 1873 the reorganization was accomplished.[59]

1. The county boards of directors were done away with, and their powers were placed largely in the hands of the boards of supervisors.

2. The powers of the county superintendent were extended; he was required to visit schools and to devote his whole time to the office. He received in compensation for his services a fixed salary instead of a *per diem*.[60]

3. The plan of taxation was changed. The teachers' fund, which had been levied by the counties, was made a state tax. The amount of the levy was fixed at four mills, and the fund was to be distributed to the counties in proportion to the number of educable children.

4. Local trustees were to be elected by a mass meeting of the patrons of the school district. They were given power to hire teachers, to look after the building, and to arbitrate between pupils and teacher.

5. Schools were to be classified as First Grade and Second Grade by the county superintendent. The monthly salaries of teachers of the second-grade schools were to be not less than $35 nor more than $60. Teachers of first-grade schools were to receive not less than $60, nor more than $75, except in the case of principals of schools of three or more teachers.

The Curriculum. The Reconstructionists were firmly of the opinion that the abolition of illiteracy was the only sure road to a strong and healthy body politic. Hence the means adopted for the improvement of the social status of the 'poor white' and Negro races was the generally accepted traditional curriculum of the day. The 'common English branches' formed the basis of the course. In the higher schools, rhetoric, Latin, astronomy, and algebra were the chief studies.[61]

The only thing regarding the curriculum that can be learned from the law creating the public school system, is that the Bible

[59] Acts of 1873, Chap. I.
[60] This salary varied from $300 per annum in Greene County to $1,800 in Hinds and Warren. The next legislature found it necessary to cut this schedule considerably.
[61] Since there has been almost no public education of secondary grade for Negroes in Mississippi, the elementary curriculum alone will be examined here.

should not be excluded from the schools.[62] The same provision was retained when the laws were recodified by the southern whites in 1878.

According to the Acts of 1873[63] second-grade schools should teach orthography, reading, penmanship, English grammar, geography, and the rudiments of arithmetic; and first-grade schools, in addition to the foregoing subjects, should teach United States history and English composition. Despite the law requiring counties to adopt uniform texts, a large variety of text-books found their way into the schools. Superintendent Cardoza in 1875 reported[64] an interesting list of the books being used in one of the counties. It may well be given in full:

> Spellers—Webster's, Union, and Holmes'.
> Readers—Wilson's, McGuffey's, Sanders', and Holmes'.
> Geographies—Mitchell's, Murray's, and Monteith's.
> Histories—Anderson's, Quackenbos', Goodrich's, and Holmes'.
> Grammars—Smith's, Butler's, Kerl's, Ingraham's, and Pinnee's.
> Arithmetics—Davies', Robinson's, and Venable's.

Several of these texts continued in use until well along into the nineties. There were frequent complaints and numerous changes. Anderson's History in particular was a mark for criticism.[65] It was claimed that this book gave the northern version of the cause of the Civil War, and that the white children were being taught to turn against the principles of their fathers.

Public oral examination of the pupils by citizens of the community was a feature of the day in both white and colored schools. A 'Conservative' writing of one such examination at the colored school at Dry Grove, gives the following account:[66]

> The exercises began with the singing of a hymn by the children, followed by the reading of a chapter from the Bible, and prayer by a colored preacher. Several of the white neighbors were present, and two of them conducted the examination by invitation of the head of the school. The children were 'put through' a course of spelling, in which the competition was very interesting and exciting to the spectators. They were examined on the elements

---

[62] Laws of 1870, Chap. I, Section 50.
[63] Acts of 1873, Chap. I, Section 22.
[64] Report of Superintendent, 1875, p. 5.
[65] Hinds County *Gazette*, March 22, 1871, quotes the Senatobia *Times*.
[66] *Ibid.*, July 5, 1876.

of arithmetic, and geography. The result of the examination was a pleasant surprise to all present.

The southern people were suspicious of northern teachers, particularly those who were employed in Negro schools. These teachers were frequently charged with teaching the Negroes false political creeds, and doctrines of social equality.[67] Such charges were frequent when the schools were first being organized. The *Gazette* humorously reported also the rumor that the Hinds County superintendent would require all children to use the 'Yankee intonation'.[68]

State Superintendent Gathright, upon assuming the duties of his office, immediately after the carpet-bag government had been dethroned, issued a circular to county superintendents, giving the views of the new administration on the subject of Negro education.[69] With respect to the aims to be accomplished he said:

Impress your teachers with the duty of instructing the colored children in the obligations they owe to society, and the responsibility imposed upon each individual of the community to maintain good morals and good order.

We find here expressed, in part, the end to be accomplished in Negro schools as seen from the standpoint of a representative southern white man. I do not think the Reconstructionists would have expressed it differently, and possibly the means employed to accomplish social improvement under both régimes differed very little. I imagine that teachers under the new administration continued using the same texts and teaching morals as they had learned them from their fathers, the political point of view in each case making very little difference.

Cardoza's Administration. Thomas W. Cardoza, a Negro already under indictment for embezzlement, succeeded Superintendent Pease as head of the school system in 1873. In the several reports issued during the period of his incumbency he called attention to the growing sentiment in favor of public schools. These reports, however, abound with references to disturbances in the school system. The revised school code had met in some degree the protests against the expensive machinery of administration, but it had bred a multitude of ills that had not been foreseen. Boards of super-

[67] Hinds County *Gazette*, March 15, 1871, quotes the Jackson *Clarion*.
[68] *Ibid.*, June 26, 1871.
[69] The Brookhaven *Ledger*, May 4, 1876.

visors, into whose hands had fallen a large share of the duties formerly assigned to the boards of directors, sometimes refused to levy taxes for the salary of the county superintendents and for school purposes.[70] Sometimes they assumed the duty of selecting texts. Local trustees insisted upon appointing teachers, and furnished "endless turmoil" in other ways.[71] County superintendents were thwarted in their efforts to administer the affairs in their counties; besides the pay in some counties was so small that properly equipped men could not be secured for the place; a bill carrying some Republican following was introduced in the Senate in 1875, which proposed to abolish the office altogether.[72] This restlessness and discontent was a forecast of the gathering storm which was soon to sweep the Republicans out of power.

The superintendent's plan to meet these disorders lay in greater centralization. He opposed efforts of the legislature to make the office of county superintendent elective.[73] Instead, he favored extending the powers of superintendents, so as to allow them to appoint teachers and select texts. In 1874, he proposed a system of district superintendents to take the place of county superintendents in sparsely settled sections of the state, which officers should have supervision over areas larger than the county.[74]

In this connection it might be well to mention certain efforts that were being made to have a compulsory education law passed. Superintendent Pease had devoted sixteen pages of his report in 1872 to a discussion of what he called "obligatory education."[75] He began his discussion with the statement that out of 400,000 educable children in the state, only 200,000 were in the schools. It is hard to determine from his treatment of the subject whether the children out of school belonged to aristocratic, poor white, or Negro families, but he seems to have had reference mainly to the poor white children.

Governor Adelbert Ames in 1874 recommended that compulsory education be studied with a view to legislative action.[76] Cardoza

[70] Superintendent's Report, 1876, p. 28.
[71] *Ibid.*, 1874, p. 9.
[72] *Weekly Pilot*, January 16, 1875.
[73] Superintendent's Report, 1874, p. 6.
[74] United States Commissioner's Report, 1874, p. 229.
[75] House Journal, 1873, p. 740.
[76] Inaugural Address, 1874.

also favored the suggestion. In fact, the Reconstructionists seem to have been fairly of one mind on the subject. The *Weekly Pilot*,[77] their chief political organ, declared in favor of it. John R. Lynch in a speech in Congress, endorsing the Civil Rights Bill, argued in favor of the compulsory education clause. [78]

[77] *Weekly Pilot*, March 6, 1875.
[78] *Ibid.*, February 20, 1875.

CHAPTER V

EDUCATION UNDER SOUTHERN RULE
1876–1886

Overturning the Republican Government. In the elections of the fall of 1875, the Democrats secured control of the legislature and in the spring of the next year they proceeded to overturn the entire Republican régime. On February 11, 1876, impeachment charges were preferred against State Superintendent Cardoza and other state officials,[1] including Governor Ames. Cardoza was charged among other things with having violated his oath when he assumed office under indictment for embezzlement, and with having misappropriated funds belonging to the normal department of Tougaloo University. Rather than face the charges Cardoza resigned from office, March 22, 1876. On April 4, Governor Stone appointed Thomas S. Gathright, a southern private schoolmaster, to fill the vacancy.

The Reconstruction government left the finances of the state in a pitiable condition.[2] The treasury had been drained, the country had been flooded with state securities worth scarcely fifty cents on the dollar, and the credit abroad had been sadly impaired. A policy of rigid economy and retrenchment had to be adopted. The school laws, passed by the legislature of 1876, had in view the curtailment of expenses. They certainly did not have in view the wrecking of the public school system and the abandonment of Negro education. Yet, as a result of these laws, the efficiency of the system was greatly reduced. The salaries of county superintendents were cut to a fifth of the schedule adopted in 1874;[3] and the salaries of teachers were fixed at figures considerably lower than they had been.[4] Teachers in schools with an average daily attendance of twenty-five or more pupils were to receive a maximum of $45 a month; teachers

---

[1] Mississippi Impeachment Trials. The caption of the present chapter was adopted in order to draw a sharp distinction between the Reconstruction government and the new government which was more truly representative of the southern population.
[2] See page 41.
[3] Laws of Mississippi, 1876, Chap. CXIII, Section 1.
[4] *Ibid.*, Section 2.

in schools with a smaller average attendance were to receive a maximum of eight cents per day for each pupil in actual attendance. It was specifically stated that state and county school funds should be used for no purposes other than the salaries of teachers and county superintendents.[5] No fund was provided for the building of schoolhouses. Every school in the county was to have equal claim upon the school funds so far as they went.[6] This provision effectually prevented any effort that might be made to run the white schools for longer terms and with higher salaried teachers than were provided for the Negro schools.

The school bill was one of the most important measures that came before the legislature at this meeting. The Democratic press seems to have endorsed the action which was taken. The *Gazette* stated that compromises had to be made in order to get the bill passed, but that it insured a better and cheaper school system, and "perfect equality of privileges and rights as between the races."[7] The Republicans, however, declared that the Democrats had destroyed the schools.[8]

Abundant proof that the Democrats did not have in mind the destruction of the school system is furnished in the statement of the Democratic leader, General J. Z. George, issued in an open letter in September, 1876.[9] He said:

If there is any one thing which the Democrats and Conservatives of this state are more determined to carry out than another, it is to provide the means of educating every child in the state, of whatever race or color. The people of Mississippi have suffered enough already from ignorance and its consequences, blind prejudices in governmental affairs, and they will not refuse to use any means in their power to remove them.

In this connection we might quote Governor Stone's sentiment, as expressed in his inaugural address, 1877:[10]

Our prosperity and greatness as a state, and happiness as a people, depend upon free and liberal education of the youth of both races.

Superintendent Gathright laid a vigorous hand upon the duties of his office. On April 25 he sent out a circular of instructions to

[5] Laws of Mississippi, Chap. CXIII, Section 3.
[6] *Ibid.*, Section 5.
[7] Hinds County *Gazette*, February 22, 1876; April 26.
[8] *Ibid.*, October 18, 1876.
[9] *Ibid.*
[10] Message, 1877, p. 11.

the county superintendents.[11]   These officers were Republican appointees.   He told them candidly that he would act upon their resignations in case they did not care to perform the duties of their office on the new salary schedule.   He explained that the cut in the salaries of superintendents and teachers was necessary.   He bade them to be rigid in the examination of teachers, and to insist that teachers devote at least six hours a day to school duties.   In respect to the education of the Negro he expressed himself in no uncertain terms:

> The state superintendent is impressed with the conviction that our highest duty to the state, to humanity, and to posterity lies in this field.   Be careful about the teachers you certify to these people.   They should have good teachers and good teaching.   It would be very gratifying to see our young men and young women, who have been well raised and carefully educated, and who are seeking employment, give themselves to work, the rewards of which will be the same in money as in the white schools, with the additional compensation of contributing to the calls of a pure philanthropy.
>
> The future of this country depends largely upon the future of the colored population, and the common schools are, and must be, the means of their elevation as they are the hope of this people.   Impress your teachers with the duty of instructing the colored children in the obligations they owe to society, and the responsibility imposed upon each individual of the community to maintain good morals and good order.

Mr. Gathright did not remain in office long enough to carry out the program which he outlined.   In the summer of the same year in which he received his appointment, he was called to the presidency of the Texas Agricultural and Mechanical College.[12]   He was succeeded by Dr. Joseph Bardwell (September 1, 1876), a "gentleman of intelligence and refinement, peculiarly fitted for the position."[13]

The laws of 1876 badly crippled the school system, yet they did much to place it upon a cash basis.   State warrants which had formerly been issued to teachers, now rose from below fifty cents on the dollar almost to par value.[14]   The loss in efficiency caused by reducing the salaries of county superintendents was felt at once.

[11] The Brookhaven *Ledger*, May 4, 1876.
[12] *Weekly Clarion*, April 3, 1878.
[13] Message of Governor Stone, 1877.
[14] Governor's Message, January 8, 1878.

The next year, Superintendent Bardwell recommended that these salaries be increased, and that the superintendents be required to visit and inspect the schools.[15] He further recommended that the salaries of teachers be based upon the grade of certificate—the plan used by the Reconstructionists—in order that first-grade teachers might earn more than the legal maximum of $45 a month. The next legislature, however, seems to have taken no cognizance of these recommendations except to permit ten 'black counties' to pay the teachers in schools with enrolments less than twenty-five, a monthly salary of $40.[16]

Opposition to the school system seems almost to have died out by this time. Superintendent Bardwell reported to the United States Commissioner of Education in 1876 that the disorders which had attended the establishment of the school system had passed away, and that "the benefit of an educated rather than an ignorant laboring class is now realized."[17] Governor Stone was able to say in 1878: "In no section of the state is there any opposition to the education of the youth of both races."[18] The State Teachers' Association in 1877 adopted a resolution of the Committee on Higher Education,[19] which had in view the organization of public high schools for the white race, and the articulation of these institutions with the elementary schools and the state university. The committee recommended also that similar schools be established for the Negroes, as soon as they were prepared for them. The fact that four of the thirty-four members of the association were Negroes seems to indicate harmony between the races with respect to educational interests.

During the period of readjustment the Negro schools were the chief sufferers. The number of educable children, between the years 1876 and 1877, showed a decrease for the white race of 20,000, and for the colored race a decrease of 10,000. This decrease was probably due to a faulty method of taking the school census, and should cause us to make large reservations in the consideration of other statistics for this year. The number of children enrolled in

---

[15] United States Commissioner's Report, 1876–1877, p. xxvii.
[16] Laws of 1877, Chap. LXXXV.
[17] United States Commissioner's Report, 1875–1876, p. 222.
[18] Governor's Message, January, 1878.
[19] Proceedings, State Teachers' Association, 1877.

the white schools showed a substantial increase, but the number in colored schools showed a decrease from 90,178 to 76,154, a loss of fifteen per cent. in one year. At the same time, the average monthly enrolment in colored schools showed a decrease from 68,580 to 44,627, or nearly thirty per cent.; the number of teachers in these schools dropped from 2,109 to 1,459, almost thirty per cent. The returns for 1876 represent only sixty-five counties, ten failing to report, but the comparison here made—with due reservation for faulty methods of computing statistics—indicates that the Negro schools were greatly demoralized by the return to power of the southern whites.[20] This may be accounted for by the fact that many northern teachers left the state at this time, leaving many schools without teachers.

The statistics indicate a return to something like normal condition in 1878. It took the Negro schools, however, until 1879 to get back to the status of 1875 with respect to the number of teachers. From this date until 1886, statistics for white and colored schools moved in parallel lines.

The Revision of the School Code, 1878. The changes made in the laws in 1876 were emergency measures designed chiefly to curtail the expenditures of the school system. They furnished a heroic remedy, but possibly the best that could be administered under the circumstances. As the laws now stood there were many conflicts, and a recodification was much needed. The object of the revision suggested in 1878 was to collect and codify, rather than to amend, the school statutes.[21]

On January 21, 1878, Representative H. A. Moody, of Panola, introduced House Bill No. 177,[22] which with a few modifications became a law on March 5. During the discussion in the House there is nothing recorded that indicates that the legislature was not as zealous for the interests of the Negroes as for the interests of the white race.

The new law preserved in all essential features the organization of the school system bequeathed by the Reconstructionists. The duties of the school officers were enumerated in detail. The county superintendency was continued as an appointive office, and a

[20] See statistical tables, p. 139.
[21] *Weekly Clarion*, February 20, 1878.
[22] House Journal, 1878.

new salary schedule set the office upon a more secure basis. The remuneration offered, however, was not sufficient to support a man devoting his whole time to it.[23] The smallness of the salary did not stand in the way of the enumeration of the duties of the office to the twenty-second item.

Other interesting features of the school laws were as follows:[24]

1. Towns of 1,000 inhabitants might be organized into separate districts.

2. No two schools of the same color were to be located nearer together than two and one-half miles, unless there was an impassable barrier between them.

3. In case the state school fund did not amount to $200,000 a year, the legislature authorized the appropriation of a sum sufficient to bring the fund up to this amount.

4. A school term of five months was authorized, provided that the county tax levy to support this did not exceed $7.50 per $1,000. A four-month term was mandatory in all counties, but there was no provision made in the case of counties in which the maximum tax levy would not support the schools for this length of time.

5. By specifying the duties of all officers in detail, overlapping of authority was avoided. For instance, supervisors could no longer select texts.

6. Counties were forbidden to levy taxes for schoolhouses.

Two points are especially interesting from the standpoint of Negro education. First, separate schools for the races were now required by law. Second, no loophole was left whereby county officials might discriminate against the Negro by giving a shorter term.[25]

A provision which militated against Negro education was the new plan of determining the salaries of teachers. It will be recalled that the Reconstruction legislature in 1873 had adopted the plan of paying teachers according to the grade of certificate which they held. The Democratic legislature in 1876 changed this and based the pay of teachers on the average daily attendance of the schools in which they taught. The new law combined the two plans. First-grade teachers were to be paid eight cents a day for each pupil in schools of an average attendance of twenty-five or more; second-grade teachers were to be paid six and a half cents for each pupil

[23] The following yearly salaries are illustrative: Adams County, $600; Hinds, $400; Washington, $350; Greene and Wayne, $45; Pearl, $40.
[24] Laws of 1878, Chap. XIV, p. 89.
[25] Laws of 1878, Chap. XIV, Section 35.

in schools of this class; and third-grade teachers were to receive only five cents a pupil. An elaborate schedule was worked out on this plan.

Such a scheme seems at first entirely equitable. The possibility for discrimination against the Negro was offered, however, in the fact that county superintendents were permitted to examine teachers and award certificates. Under these conditions a superintendent with a small fund to distribute, or one prejudiced against the education of the Negro, might award to Negro teachers certificates based rather on the amount he wished to pay them than on the fitness of the teacher.

The Burden of Supporting the School System. The burden of supporting the school system grew increasingly heavy. Complaints were loud and deep.[26] The salaries of teachers were cut in order to maintain the mandatory term of four months.[27] Mississippi, in common with her sister states of the South, was now going through a period of unprecedented depression. The value of realty actually decreased [28] from $95,000,000 in 1876 to $88,500,000 in 1886, a loss of $6,500,000; the value of personal property increased from $35,700,000 to $40,700,000, a gain of only $5,000,000 in ten years. The commonwealth was therefore poorer than when the Reconstructionists left the state.

The school fund in 1886, including moneys received from fines, licenses, and forfeitures, amounted to but $335,551.23. As the value of property steadily declined, the demands of the schools steadily increased. During the eight years between 1876 and 1884 the school population increased about twenty-five per cent., if we may rely upon the only figures we have, which are approximately correct. Further, the enrolment in schools increased from 205,378 in 1878 to 282,733 in 1886, or about 35 per cent.

The following excerpt from the Report of the United States Commissioner gives an idea of the weight Mississippi was bearing:[29]

Mississippi with a population of 1,131,597, the school age being five to twenty-one, reports $3.65 per capita on average attendance; New Jersey, population being 1,131,116, school age being five to eighteen, reports $15.14 per capita on average attendance.

[26] Hinds County *Gazette*, January 21, 1878.
[27] Proceedings, Mississippi Teachers Association, 1883.
[28] State Auditor's Reports, 1876, 1886.
[29] United States Commissioner's Report, 1883–1884, p. lx.

Little as this appears to be, the state could do no more.

Such was the condition in this and other southern states when a committee of the Peabody trustees memorialized Congress to give national aid toward the education of the Negro in these states.[30] Business depression, the burden of illiteracy, and the slow recovery of the state from the devastation of war and reconstruction, it was declared, made even small tax levies exceedingly onerous.

Was there a tendency of the ruling class to take for themselves a larger share of the school funds than in equity fell to their lot? We have seen that the laws of 1878 did not permit discrimination against the Negro in respect to the length of the school term. There was, however, a loophole for discrimination in respect to the salaries of teachers. For the decade 1876 to 1886 the reports of the state superintendent make no distinction between the salaries of white and colored teachers, so statistics throw no light on the subject.

The narrative reports of the county superintendents furnish only slight evidence that discrimination was even desired. The superintendent of De Soto County admitted[31] that a few citizens in that county opposed the teaching of Negro institutes on the ground that the teachers would thereby be improved, and would thus have to be awarded higher certificates and larger salaries. That the opposition was not pronounced is shown by the fact that the same superintendent was teaching a Negro institute two months in the year.

The superintendent of Warren County explained the situation in his county as follows:[32]

There are about ten Negro children to one white going to school in the county, while in the city (Vicksburg) there is little difference in the number. The proportion of taxes paid by the white and colored citizens of the city and county, is as eight to one, about. I am in favor of dividing the school funds equally among the races. We receive from all sources $11,000 for school purposes; to divide this so that a fund of $5,000 should be for the white children, and the same amount for the colored, would give the former six or eight months' schooling, and the latter two months.

These bits of evidence show that the burden of supporting schools for Negroes was beginning to make the tax-payers restive. The increasing popularity of the public schools for the whites, and

[30] Proceedings, Peabody Fund, vol. ii, p. 270.
[31] Superintendent's Report, 1882–1883, Narrative Report of De Soto County.
[32] *Ibid.*, 1884–1885, Narrative Report of Warren County.

the consequent demand for funds to bring them to a higher state of efficiency, probably contributed to this spirit.

The Efficiency of the System. The first decade after the return to southern rule is characterized by growing popularity of the public school system, indicated by the rapid increase in the enrolment and average attendance in the schools, and by the increase in the number of teachers and the number of schools.[33] The progress of schools for both races is almost parallel. This rapid growth, however, is marked by a very low degree of efficiency. The length of term for country schools averaged less than seventy-eight days, and for town schools, about one hundred and fifty-five days. A four-months' session was divided into two terms, one of which was taught in the winter, and the other in mid-summer.[34] The school law required that no two schools of the same color should be established nearer together than two and one-half miles, yet, notwithstanding this, a larger number of schools were established than could be supported by the available funds.[35] Counties had to go into debt to meet their obligations and were forced to ask the legislature to pass local relief acts.

The efficiency of the county superintendents was of a very low order. Few received a salary higher than $300 a year in 1885; the maximum annual salary was $1,000 in Adams County, and the minimum was $60 in Jones and Quitman.[36] They were of course permitted to pursue other vocations in addition to performing the duties of their office. Important duties were by law entrusted to these officers, but it was not expected that they devote more than a small part of their time to them. State Superintendent Smith had repeatedly recommended to the legislature that the salary schedule be raised, but no substantial increase was made. There was consequently no supervision, and little inspection worthy of the name.[37] The certification of teachers was lax, and often certificates were granted to any teacher who needed a place. In consequence of laxity and neglect, Negro schools suffered in common with the white.

[33] See statistical tables, p. 139; also Peabody Reports, Vol. III, p. 162.
[34] Report of Superintendent, 1886–1887, p. 5.
[35] *Ibid.*, 1886–1887 p. 13.
[36] *Ibid.*, 1884–1885, Statistics.
[37] *Ibid.*, 1886–1887, p. 1; Proceedings, Mississippi Teachers' Association, 1883.

The Teaching Body. In 1879 five teachers' institutes were held in the state, aided by a contribution of $1,000 from the Peabody Fund. The Peabody Board continued to aid these institutes until 1884, when, on account of the repudiation by the state of the Planters' Bank bonds, the contribution was withdrawn.[38] The low requirements for certification, and the laxity of county superintendents, had not made for a very high degree of efficiency in teachers. The superintendent in 1887 thus summarized the situation:

> Nearly 6,000 teachers are employed annually, and it is safe to say that less than 1,000 of these have had any professional training. One thousand more come yearly into the schools without one day's experience; while fully one-third of the corps are using the vocation as a temporary means of a livelihood, or a stepping-stone to a more remunerative occupation.[39]

There was no normal school for whites, and the chair of pedagogy was not established in the university till some years later. White teachers could secure professional training only by leaving the state or by availing themselves of the meager provisions of the institutes. It is true that a few scholarships were provided at George Peabody College, but these were revoked in 1884.

Negro teachers were much better provided for. The Normal Department of Tougaloo University, maintained by the state since 1872, was turning out a very high grade of teacher, but the disagree-

---

[38] In George Peabody's first bequest were included bonds of the state of Mississippi, issued to the Planters' Bank before the war. Mr. Peabody estimated that the value of these bonds on the date of the bequest was eleven hundred thousand dollars. Their validity had been confirmed by the legislature and the supreme court of the state. The trustees sent a memorial to the Reconstruction legislature, requesting payment of bonds and interest. No response of any sort was received (vol. 1, pp. 274, 279). The finance committee of the trustees had the matter continuously in their hands from 1871 to 1873, but no aggressive action was taken other than what has been mentioned. Mr. T. S. Manning was authorized in 1881 to take the matter up with the state authorities, and press for the payment. He was, however, assured by Governor Stone that a constitutional amendment, passed in 1876, prohibited the settlement of the indebtedness. Notwithstanding this answer, Judge Manning presented the matter to the legislature the next year. His memorial was referred to the Judiciary Committee, "where it slept." In 1884 he informed the trustees that there was not the slightest chance that the state would recognize its obligation, and recommended that Mississippi be stricken from the list of beneficiaries of the Peabody Fund. Up to this date the state had received nearly $70,000 from the fund. The state was unanimously restored to the right to participate in the benefits of the trust, October, 1892.

[39] Superintendent's Report, 1886–1887, p. 1.

ment of the trustees of the normal department with representatives of the American Missionary Association which controlled the university, caused the legislature of 1879 to withhold its appropriation for two years.[40] The misunderstanding was soon adjusted and the state continued its support. The enrolment in the university for 1884–1885 was 219. The normal department was conducted by a principal and two assistants. The curriculum was composed largely of secondary school subjects. There were also a theological department and industrial departments of the university.[41]

The State Normal School at Holly Springs was established by an act of the legislature, July 20, 1870, for the training of colored teachers. The Reconstruction government had appropriated from $4,500 to $5,000 a year for maintenance. The southern government continued the yearly appropriation but cut it down to $3,000. The high-water mark in the enrolment was reached in 1880, when 220 students were registered. The average enrolment for the period with which we are dealing, lay somewhere between 125 and 150. Up to 1887 the course embraced four years. Theory and practice, music, and the traditional secondary subjects seem to have formed the basis of the curriculum.[42]

In addition to these institutions may be mentioned Alcorn Agricultural and Mechanical College for Negroes. Of Alcorn, as an institution for the training of teachers, Governor Lowry in 1884 has this to say:[43]

Most of the students who are sufficiently advanced, engage in teaching when they leave college, and one-fourth of those in attendance now have taught at different times in the public schools. The college is practically a normal school for the education of colored teachers, though agriculture is taught with some success, except that few students ever engage seriously in farming. Nearly all educated negroes are inclined to teaching.

Alcorn College had had a very irregular and almost tempestuous career since its establishment in 1871. Bad management and political interference lay at the bottom of the troubles. Throughout

---

[40] Report of Superintendent, 1880, p. 13; Governor's Message, 1880, p. 17.

[41] I shall not attempt a detailed history of the normal schools of Mississippi.   Mayes, in his *History of Education in Mississippi*, has covered the ground with a fair degree of thoroughness.

[42] Mayes: *History of Education in Mississippi*.

[43] Governor's Message, 1884, p. 11.

its history, up to this time, the attendance had been broken and irregular, few pupils remaining through the entire session. The yearly enrolment was about 125. The statute which reorganized Alcorn in 1878 provided for an institution where the colored youth "might acquire a common school education and a scientific and practical knowledge of agriculture," etc.

These three institutions were training a considerable number of teachers during the period. It must be remembered, however, that their contribution was relatively small; further, that they had to draw their patronage from the pupils in country schools where meager advantages were provided, and, consequently, that their curricula had to be kept within reach of the public schools. These were practically the only public secondary schools for Negroes. In conclusion, we may say that the level of the teaching profession, so far as colored schools were concerned, was necessarily low.

The Curriculum. At a meeting of the State Teachers' Association in 1877 a committee on higher education presented a two-page report suggesting a system of secondary schools which would connect the elementary schools with the university.[44] The last paragraph of this report reveals the attitude of the representative southern white teachers with respect to the ideal of an educational 'ladder' for the colored race:

> What has been said in regard to the provision for white children coming up through the line of common schools, high schools, and a great university, should be applied as soon as they are prepared for it, to a similar line of progress for colored children.

The legislature in 1878 established a system of secondary schools in accordance with the foregoing recommendation by permitting students in certain specially qualified academies to draw a *pro rata* of the state funds from their county treasuries.[45] This provision probably applied only in the case of white students. It was later declared unconstitutional.

In the revision of the school laws in 1878 the curriculum was not specified. In later years, the subjects required for teacher's examination constituted the curriculum, so it may safely be inferred that, at this date, although not stated by law, these were the

[44] Proceedings, State Teachers' Association, 1877.
[45] Laws of 1878, Chap. XX.

subjects taught in the schools. The requirements for examination were as follows:[46]

FIRST GRADE	SECOND GRADE	THIRD GRADE
Higher branches of English Literature	Intermediate Arithmetic	Elementary Arithmetic
Natural Philosophy	Geography	Spelling
Elements of Bookkeeping	Grammar	Reading
"All studies usually taught in the common schools"	Spelling	Writing
	Reading	
	Writing	

The State Teachers' Association in 1882 recommended [47] that elementary algebra, composition and rhetoric, and the history and practice of teaching be substituted for natural philosophy and the "higher branches of English literature," as subjects required for examination. The legislature, however, seems to have taken no cognizance of the matter until 1886. We may infer that the subjects listed constituted, in the main, the course of study in the public schools.

There was a statute requiring each county to adopt uniform texts, but since there was no penalty attached, it was but indifferently observed. Many of the old-time texts doubtless continued in use. Webster's "Blue-back Speller," used in 1873, was still in use in 1886.

For the most part, we may say the curriculum was formal, particularly so in the elementary school. In the upper grades, natural philosophy, bookkeeping, and literature show a tendency toward content subjects, but in Negro public schools it is doubtful if these subjects were reached by any except a few of the most persistent pupils.

[46] Laws of 1878, Chap. XIV, Section 27.
[47] Report of Superintendent, 1882–1883, p. 4.

CHAPTER VI

THE DEVELOPMENT OF THE PUBLIC SCHOOL
SYSTEM SINCE 1886

In the four succeeding chapters I shall undertake to trace the development of the public school system since 1886. These four chapters might well be included under the caption of the present chapter, but for the fact that it is necessary to give a rather elaborate treatment of the status of the teaching body, the distribution of the state school fund, and the curriculum. It has seemed best, therefore, to treat these topics in separate chapters.

The growing popularity of the public schools in the decade just preceding this date gave rise, as we have seen, to the establishment of a large number of schools and to the enrolment of an increasingly large number of pupils. But the schools, being left in most instances to the care of ignorant, bickering, and jealous local trustees, and having virtually no supervision from the county or state, provided but meager opportunities for proper instruction. Beginning with 1886, definite efforts were made by the state department to provide some form of supervision, to improve the status of the teaching body, and to provide adequate buildings. Yet, for at least fourteen years, because of the actual poverty of the state, very little progress was made along these lines. Not until 1900 does a period of real progress begin.

For convenient treatment the quarter century embraced between the years 1886 and 1910 falls happily into two periods—first, the fourteen years of slow and almost imperceptible progress from 1886 to 1900; and second, the period of remarkable growth and prosperity embracing the last decade of our study.

The Reforms of 1886. As we have seen, the demand for public school education had grown greatly during the ten years preceding 1886, and the machinery of administration was now entirely inadequate for doing efficient service. In 1886, J. R. Preston became state superintendent. He succeeded in inducing the legislature to enact a number of sweeping reforms.

Lack of supervision was declared to be one of the chief defects of the school system.[1] The county superintendency, which had existed since Reconstruction days on a salary basis insufficient to secure more than nominal service, was now placed on firmer ground by the adoption of a new salary schedule.[2] The salary of the office was fixed at three per cent. of the total school funds received annually by the county, provided that no county pay more than $600 a year or less than $150. The minimum limit certainly worked for the advantage of the schools in counties where only forty and sixty dollars had been paid. In return for this increase in the emoluments of his office, the superintendent was required to visit and inspect the schools, and to spend the first three Saturdays of each month conducting institutes for teachers in various centers in the county.[3] Each race was to have separate institutes and each was to receive an equal share of the institute days.

Another defect was remedied by the new law in the making of the school term of four months continuous. Heretofore, it had been a frequent practice in certain parts of the state to run the schools two months in the winter and two months in mid-summer.[4] The evil of the plan is apparent. The new law permitted the local trustees to determine whether the district school should be taught during the winter months or the summer months, but required that the term be continuous. County superintendents were divided on the question whether winter or summer was the better season in which to operate the schools.[5] Poor schoolhouses, bad roads, thin clothing of pupils were arguments in favor of summer schools.

The Re-districting Law was another step toward remedying a defective system. Up to this time the county had been the unit of local organization, but the trustees of the sub-districts seem to have controlled the schools, so far as anybody controlled them. The new law made the district the unit of local organization, but left powers of general supervision, and the fixing of limits of school districts with the county board and the county superintendent.

The trouble heretofore had been that more schools were established than could be supported by the county revenues. Although,

[1] Proceedings, State Teachers' Association, 1883.
[2] Laws, 1886, Chap. XXIV, Section 16.
[3] *Ibid.*, Sections 23–26.
[4] Report of Superintendent, 1886–1887, p. 5.
[5] Proceedings, State Teachers' Association, 1887.

according to the law of 1878, schools for the same race could not be established nearer together than two and one-half miles, they seem to have been located "at the instance of every neighborhood faction."[6] Sometimes, also, a teacher living in a certain community had a school established for his own convenience. The new law did much to remedy this evil. The county board was empowered to lay off and alter the school districts, but no district was to contain less than forty-five educable children, except in cases where impassable barriers prevented such an arrangement.[7] There were separate districts for each race. Under this law, about 500 schools were closed during the first year.

Separate school districts were authorized by the law of 1878 for towns of 1,000 inhabitants. But since there were relatively few such towns in the state, the advantages of the separate district were necessarily restricted. The separate districts contained the only schools that had really flourished before 1886. Twenty-two such districts were in existence at this time.[8] In order to extend these advantages the new law permitted towns of 750 to become separate districts.

Perhaps the most important reform was the establishment of uniform examinations for teachers. Under the old plan, the examination had been hardly more than a matter of form; county superintendents often granted certificates to any who needed a place.[9] Under the new plan questions for examination were sent out from the state office, and superintendents were required to see that honest examinations were held. The subjects on which teachers were to be examined for license were as follows:[10]

FIRST GRADE	SECOND GRADE	THIRD GRADE
Spelling	Spelling	Spelling
Reading	Reading, to fifth	Reading, to fifth reader
Mental and Practical	reader	Primary Mental Arith-
Arithmetic	Mental Arithmetic	metic
Geography	Practical Arithmetic,	Rudiments of practical
English Grammar	to cube root	Arithmetic through
Composition	Geography (elementary)	fractions and simple
United States History	Grammar (elementary)	interest
Natural Philosophy	Composition	Geography (elementary)
(elementary)	Primary United States	Primary Language Lessons
Elementary Physiology	History	

In addition to passing a satisfactory examination on these subjects, applicants were required to furnish evidence of good moral character and ability to manage a school.

The grade of certificate was made the basis for determining the limits of salaries for teachers. Formerly the average daily attendance in the school was taken into consideration also, but the abuse of the plan led to its abolition. The salary for third-grade teachers was fixed between the limits $15 and $20; for second-grade teachers, between $18 and $30; for first-grade, between $25 and $55. In determining the exact salary of a particular teacher, the county superintendent was required to take into consideration the size of the school and the executive ability of the teacher.

The new law also placed the school finances on a more stable basis. The state treasurer was authorized, in case the school fund did not amount to $300,000 *per annum*, to transfer an amount from the treasury sufficient to make up the balance. A county tax of three mills was made mandatory.[11]

Up to this time the administration of the schools had been placed largely in the hands of the county boards of supervisors, who looked after the school interests along with other public interests such as the building of bridges and up-keep of roads. The new law required that the county superintendent with the advice of the supervisors should appoint a county school board. One board member was to be appointed from each supervisor's district to serve a term of two years, and was to be exempt from road and jury service. The superintendent was *ex-officio* president of the board. The county board was vested with general supervision of the schools, with power to determine the limits of sub-districts, etc.

The trustees of the districts were not overlooked in the general revision of the school laws.[12] It was required that at least one member should be able to read and write, and that two should be residents of the district in which the school was located.

[6] Report of Superintendent, 1886–1887, p. 5.

[7] Laws of 1886, Chap. XXIV, Section 40.

[8] Report of Superintendent, 1901–1903.

[9] *Ibid.*, 1886–1887, p. 4.

[10] Laws of 1886–1887, Chap. XXIV, Sections 49–53.

[11] *Ibid.*, Section 67.

[12] *Ibid.*, Section 26.

As is always the case in the inauguration of reforms, there was at first widespread criticism and complaint. Grounds for complaint were found chiefly in the uniform examinations and in the re-districting law. In a short time, however, this died away, and the people began to see the beneficent results of the new system. Governor Lowry in 1889 characterized the change which had taken place in public opinion, as "a significant triumph" for the state superintendent.[13]

The Material Equipment of the Schools. One of the most crying needs of the school system was the need of better buildings and furnishings. The abuses of local taxation to which the Reconstructionists had been led in their efforts to provide school equipment, had taught the tax-payers a bitter lesson, and one which they did not soon forget. The Democrats, as soon as they came into power, withdrew from the counties the right to tax themselves for this purpose. And as the resources of the state were still at a low ebb, the legislature had not dared to make an appropriation for schoolhouses.

For want of statistics to indicate the true condition of the school equipment, I have drafted from the narrative reports of the county superintendents (Report of State Superintendent, 1886–1887) a summary which gives a vague outline of the situation. These reports are in many cases incomplete and lacking in definiteness, so we can but take the data they offer and infer what we may.

1. Counties in which there were no log schoolhouses: Washington and Warren.

2. Counties which had eliminated all except a few log houses: Adams, Madison, and Lowndes.

3. Counties in which it is definitely stated that half the buildings were log houses: Alcorn, Attala, Calhoun, Clay, Hinds, Jasper, Panola, Prentiss, and Wilkinson.

4. Counties in which at least two-thirds of the buildings were log houses: Greene, Itawamba, Lauderdale, Marion, Neshoba, Perry, and Wayne.

5. Total number of counties reporting, sixty-eight.

This additional information has been derived from the reports: Eighteen superintendents reported that churches were being used, particularly by the Negroes, in the absence of buildings provided by public expense. Desks were in use in but eighteen counties, and

[13] Governor's Message, 1889, p. 9.

split-log benches were still used in at least one county. Thirty-one superintendents, in describing the condition of the school-houses, employed such terms as, 'bad', 'wretched', 'deplorable', 'shockingly destitute'.

It is not difficult to see that the condition of schoolhouses was far from good, and we may easily infer that those for Negroes were worse than those for whites. It is true that in many counties Negroes made extensive use of their churches, but these, aside from being poorly adapted for school purposes, could scarcely be called comfortable.

The large number of log houses astounds one used to the conveniences of these latter days. We may say that the average schoolhouse in 1886 was a poorly lighted frame shanty, heated by a smoky stove, and equipped with rude benches or home-made desks; through large cracks in the walls and floor the drafts of winter were permitted to play upon the poorly clad children.

The interest in public schools which had been rapidly growing for ten years, and which culminated in the reforms of 1886, inspired the people in their efforts to secure a better equipment. Between 1887 and 1889, 826 new buildings were constructed at a cost of $330,000. There is no means of determining how many of these were built for colored children, but it is safe to say that not all were built for the white population.

In 1888–1889 the 'Two and Three Per Cent. Fund', which under an act of the legislature in 1882 had been allowed to accumulate to this date, was distributed to the counties to be applied to buildings and repairs.[14] Unfortunately, the legislature did not specify the conditions under which the fund was to be disbursed to the school districts. The state superintendent advised the district trustees to supplement their shares of the fund but in many places this was not done, and in some places the trustees unlawfully applied the money to the payment of teachers. However, from a fund amounting to $78,429.05, about 500 buildings were erected.

From 1888 to 1895, country schools to the number of 2,348 were built, or more than a third as many as were needed. The majority of these were well-constructed frame buildings and afforded "reasonable accommodations" for the children.[15] The towns, in the

[14] Report of Superintendent, 1888–1889, p. 8.
[15] *Ibid.*, 1893–1895, p. 43.

meantime, constructed twenty-five brick buildings costing from $10,000 to $30,000 each, and twenty-three frame buildings costing from $2,500 to $8,000 each.

The right of district trustees to change the location of the schools was a deterrent factor which prevented many communities from building permanent houses.[16] Despite the efforts put forth to improve the equipment of schools, comparatively little seems to have been accomplished. The superintendent in 1900 said:

> Our schoolhouses, as a rule, are a disgrace to the state. They are not adapted for the work for which they were erected; as a rule, no attention being paid to the proper lighting, heating, sanitation, and architecture. I do not believe there is a neighborhood in the state too poor to build a comfortable and well-arranged house.[17]

Material Equipment, 1900–1910. Table III tells about all there is to say in regard to the material equipment for this period. From it we learn that not less than 2,135 schoolhouses were built during this decade, and that the number built for use of the white population exceeded by three to one the number built for Negroes. The fact that local funds and private subscriptions provided the chief means for the erection of buildings, accounts for this difference in numbers for each race.

Superintendent Whitfield devoted a large part of his energy from 1900 to 1905 toward improving the material equipment of the schools. He published detailed directions for the location of schools, for erection of buildings, and for proper lighting, heating, and ventilation.[18] He attributed the low average attendance (scarcely sixty per cent.) to disability of pupils, caused by defects in the school equipment. Speaking of the condition of the schoolhouses, he says:

> It is unnecessary to give statistics in regard to the condition of the rural schoolhouses of the state. That they are in the main uncomfortable and unsightly and wholly inadequate for their purposes is admitted by everyone.

The superintendent doubtless had in mind the rural schools for whites when he made the foregoing statement. If such was the condition of white schoolhouses, what must have been the condition of the buildings for Negroes?

[16] Report of Superintendent, 1898–1899, p. 4.
[17] *Ibid.*, 1899–1901, p. 1.
[18] *Ibid.*, 1901–1903; 1903–1905.

However, there was unquestionably much improvement during the decade, at least so far as the white schools were concerned. The first annual report of the Rural School Supervisor contains a survey of the conditions.[19] He sums up the situation with respect to buildings in the following words:

> In the matter of equipment in the way of buildings and furniture great improvements have been made within recent years, but there remains much to be done to make the equipment adequate to meet the needs of the country children. It seems that about seventy per cent. of the rural schoolhouses are still unpainted, while many are uncomfortable and poorly lighted.[20]

TABLE III

SCHOOLHOUSES AND COST OF BUILDINGS—1899, 1900, AND 1909

	SCHOOLHOUSES BUILT		EXPENDITURE FOR BUILDINGS BY STATE
	White	*Colored*	
1899–1900	166[21]	58[22]	
1900–1901			
1901–1902	201	97	$13,531
1902–1903	215	82	22,142
1903–1904	227	61	43,623
1904–1905	330	109	44,534
1905–1906	333	94	57,833
1906–1907	262	75	96,083
1907–1908	199	73	
1908–1909	202	75	
Total	2,135	724	277,746

[19] Report of Superintendent, 1909–1911.

[20] Marvelous strides have been made since 1910, and when the story of the last seven years has been told, the springing up of new, modern buildings will appear like the work of magic. But the colored race has by no means shared equally in this form of educational prosperity. Indeed, it is clear to a casual observer that very little progress has been made in improving the condition of Negro schools.

[21] Author's estimate from data in Superintendent's Report; schools located in fifty-three counties.

[22] Author's estimate from data in Superintendent's Report; schools located in twenty-five counties.

Educational Progress Since 1886. The type of organization adopted for the school system in 1886 is fundamentally the same that we have at present. A few minor changes have been made, but in its essential character there has been but slight modification. The immediate effect of the laws of 1886 was salutary. The uniform examination of teachers, the inspection of schools by the county superintendent, the re-districting law, the permission of communities of 750 to establish separate districts, the establishment of a county school board, all tended to promote the efficiency of the schools. It is our purpose in the succeeding pages of this chapter to follow the general trend of educational activity for the next quarter of a century.

A law [23] which caused considerable agitation among people interested in education, was a statute passed in 1890 requiring county school boards, on the recommendation of five competent teachers, to adopt uniform texts for the county. There was a widespread protest against this law, and the superintendent was called upon to enforce it through the State Department.[24] When those who opposed the law became convinced that its provisions were mandatory, and that the superintendent was determined to enforce it, opposition ceased.

Since the establishment of the system, the status of the county superintendent had been precarious. Attempts have now and then been made to abolish the office and provide for some other means of administering the duties belonging to it. Such an attempt was made in the Constitutional Convention in 1890, but it failed to gain any following.[25] From the first, there had been a considerable element in the legislative bodies which favored making the office elective. As time went on, there was a growing tendency on the part of the counties to seek from the legislature the special privilege of electing their own superintendents; in 1892, a special act permitted all counties except fourteen to do so.[26] In 1896, superintendents were elected in all counties except Adams, Coahoma, Hinds, Sunflower, Warren, and Washington.[27] Soon these six yielded to the voice of the people demanding an elective office.

[23] Annotated Code of 1892, Section 4068.
[24] Raymond *Gazette*, November 15, 29; December 13, 20, 1890.
[25] Journal of Constitutional Convention, 1890, p. 329.
[26] Laws of 1892, Chap. 131.
[27] Laws of 1896, Chap. 108.

A law of 1892 provided that every county with fifteen school districts for either race, should hold an institute for five days each scholastic year.[28] The fee of fifty cents, charged each applicant for license, was supposed to defray the expense of these institutes. This represented a great improvement over the plan provided in 1886, but it did not prove very efficient.

A county examining board was established in 1890.[29] This board consisted of the county superintendent and two first-grade teachers or college graduates, who were authorized to examine the papers of all applicants for license to teach. In 1896 the State Board of Examiners was established [30] and authorized to issue professional and state licenses. State licenses were legal for one-, two- and three-year periods, according to the per cent. of proficiency indicated on the applicant's papers. Teachers who received state licenses a second time, were granted exemption from further examination.

Separate districts were required by law in 1892 to make either or both of their schools graded schools.[31] Graded schools were defined as follows: First, graded grammar schools, in which the elementary branches were taught; and second, graded high schools, in which were provided studies for those who had passed the graded grammar school course. The trustees were permitted to fix reasonable tuition fees for high school students. Children from the country had been permitted since 1886 to attend the separate district schools, and have their *pro rata* of the school fund transferred to the separate district.

In 1906 the county board of education was empowered to establish rural separate districts [32] having an area of not less than sixteen square miles. Such districts, however, were not permitted the rights of separate districts, unless they maintained a school for seven months. The county board of supervisors levied the tax for maintenance on petition of a majority of the qualified electors.

Two years later municipal authorities were permitted to issue bonds to build and repair schoolhouses, and to maintain schools.[33]

[28] Annotated Code of 1892, Sections 99 to 102.
[29] Laws of 1890, Chap. 71, Section 8.
[30] Laws of 1896, Chap. 106.
[31] Laws of 1892, Section 4015.
[32] Annotated Code of 1906, Section 4530.
[33] Laws of 1908, Chap. 101.

In 1904, a uniform text-book law was passed [34] which permitted a commission of eight teachers appointed by the governor to select texts for use in all public schools for a period of five years. Texts in the following subjects were to be adopted: orthography, reading, writing, intellectual arithmetic, practical arithmetic, geography, English grammar, composition, United States history, physiology, civil government, elements of agriculture, history of Mississippi.

The statutory course of study was now composed of the same subjects that were required of teachers in the county examinations. The list of studies for examination, however, had been increased in 1904 by the addition of elements of agriculture.[35]

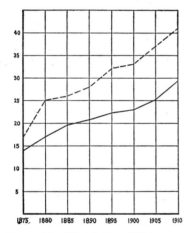 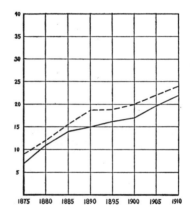

Fig. 1 School Population: White ——;
Colored – – – –. Expressed in
Ten Thousands

Fig. 2 Enrolment: White ——;
Colored – – – –. Expressed in
Ten Thousands

The trend of public sentiment was unquestionably in the direction of adapting the schools to the needs of the people. A Committee of Five was appointed by the State Teachers' Association in 1901 to investigate the conditions prevailing in rural schools and make recommendations to the association. The committee rendered an elaborate report in May, 1903.[36] Among the recommendations of the committee the most prominent were: (1) the

[34] Laws of 1904, Chap. 86.
[35] *Ibid.*
[36] Report of Superintendent, 1901–1903.

encouragement of local taxation with the county as a unit; (2) better supervision of rural schools through a county superintendent responsible to a board; (3) systematic training of teachers through normals and institutes; (4) a revision of the course of study, placing less emphasis upon mental and practical arithmetic and more on English and history; (5) the addition of agriculture on the list of statutory subjects.

Superintendent Whitfield in 1905 recommended the establishment of rural high schools, and also the establishment of a limited number of agricultural high schools. The recommendation with respect to agricultural high schools was repeated by Superintendent Powers in 1907, with the result that the legislature agreed to the establishment of one such school in each county.[37] The school so established was to receive $1,500 from the state. This law, however, was declared unconstitutional because it did not provide for the education of the colored youth. The present agricultural high school bill was passed as a substitute in 1910.[38] It provides for the establishment of one such school for the white youth and one for the colored youth in any county, after the electors of the county have voted a levy for equipment and maintenance. The two schools may be established at different times, and separate levies are to be made for each school. This means that the voters, at present practically all white, determine whether a Negro agricultural high school shall be established. The result has been that no Negro schools have as yet been established.

The consolidation of schools was a topic in the report of Superintendent Powers in 1907. The recommendation received legislative favor in 1910,[39] and county school boards were authorized to consolidate schools and to provide for the transportation of pupils.

Other steps toward the improvement of rural schools were the organization of boys' corn clubs, which became very popular in the later years of this decade, the organization of a school improvement association, and the appointment of a rural school supervisor in 1910. These movements represent strides far in advance of the faltering pace of 1900. It should be observed, however, that Negro schools have not shared to any great extent in this progress.

[37] Laws of 1908, Chap. 102.
[38] Laws of 1910, Chap. 122.
[39] *Ibid.*, Chap. 124.

Stagnation is written large in the statistics for white schools for the period embraced between 1886 and 1899. (See Table IV.) While there was a substantial increase in the enrolment and in the percentage of the school population enrolled, the average daily attendance increased but 16.0 per cent. and the number of teachers but 15.1 per cent. The enrolment was outrunning the in-

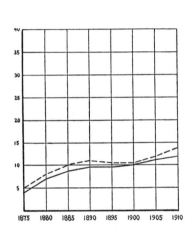

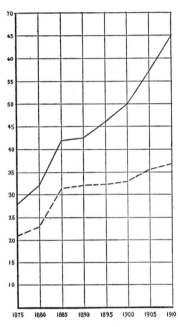

Fig. 3 *Average Daily Attendance:*
White————; *Colored* – – – –. *Expressed*
in Ten Thousands

Fig. 4 *Number of Teachers:*
White————; *Colored* – – – –. *Expressed*
in Thousands

crease in the number of teachers, so that in 1899 the average teacher (on the basis of enrolment) had to care for four more pupils than he did in 1886. For the increase in service thus required, he received a raise in salary of twenty-seven cents per month, making an average monthly salary of $31.64.

In the Negro schools for the same period positive retrogression is evident, if statistics indicate the true situation. Although the Negro school population was increasing far more rapidly than the school population of the white race, the enrolment was not keeping pace. White schools in 1899 were enrolling 10.95 per cent. more of the school population than in 1886, and the Negro schools but 5.36 per cent. more. Yet, the increase of enrolment in Negro schools was far in excess of the increase of the average daily attendance. In fact, the average daily attendance showed scarcely any increase. The number of teachers also failed to increase. In 1899, the average Negro teacher was required to teach sixty-three children, thirteen more than in 1886, and for this increase in his duties he received the sum of $19.39, or $8.01 less than he received in 1886.

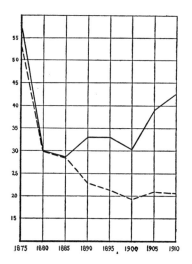

Fig. 5　*Average Monthly Salaries of Teachers:*
White ———; Colored ———.
Expressed in Dollars

In marked contrast with the depression of the period just discussed is the progress in white schools during the succeeding ten years. The enrolment increased 32.4 per cent. and the average daily attendance, 41.1 per cent. In 1909, 91.78 per cent. of the school population was being enrolled. The number of teachers increased 38 per cent., their average monthly salaries increased nearly ten dollars, and the number of pupils per teacher was slightly reduced. The schools were now reaching a larger number of people than ever before, and were developing the machinery for a higher degree of efficiency than they had ever before exhibited.

In Negro schools we see a few of the marks of progress, but we cannot say that they have advanced very far. In the last ten years there has been a substantial increase in the enrolment and average attendance. The number of teachers has increased 17.5 per cent., but has by no means kept pace with the enrolment. The average Negro teacher now has to teach four children more than he did in 1899, and receives for it ninety-two cents more a month. He is now attempting the Herculean task of teaching sixty-seven children, or almost twice as many as the average white teacher is required to teach. Were it not for the fact that such a small percentage of the enrolment is in daily attendance, colored teachers would be able to accomplish little indeed. As things now stand, we can hope for but the most meager returns.

When we consider in connection with the statistical data we have just interpreted, the fact that the average rural school term is barely four months, that the buildings used for school purposes are altogether inadequate, and that the teachers have little or no training, we need not wonder that Negroes who receive instruction in such schools continue in ignorance, shiftlessness, and crime.

TABLE IV

PROGRESS OF WHITE AND COLORED SCHOOLS, 1886 TO 1899

(*Compiled from Statistics in Reports of the State Superintendent*)

	WHITE			COLORED		
	1886	*1899*	*Per Cent. Increase*	*1886*	*1899*	*Per Cent. Increase*
School population	202,532	227,470[40]	11.7	269,090	331,330[40]	23.1
Enrolment	129,203	167,173	29.4	153,530	191,968	25.0
Per cent. of school population enrolled	62.76[41]	73.71[41]	10.95	53.45[41]	58.09[41]	5.36
Average daily attendance	84,884	98,379	16.0	99,134	102,447	3.3
Teachers	3,840	4,419	15.1	3,012	3,023	.03
Pupils per teacher[42]	33.7	37.8		50.9	63.5	
Average monthly salaries of teachers	$31.37	$31.64	$0.27[43]	$27.40	$19.39	—$8.01[43]

PROGRESS OF WHITE AND COLORED SCHOOLS, 1899 TO 1909

	WHITE			COLORED		
	1899	*1909*	*Per Cent. Increase*	*1899*	*1909*	*Per Cent. Increase*
School population	227,470[40]	241,218[40]	6.0	331,330[40]	360,925[40]	8.1
Enrolment	167,173	221,392	32.4	191,968	238,639	24.2
Per cent. of school population enrolled	73.71[41]	91.78[41]	18.07	58.09[41]	66.11[41]	8.02
Average daily attendance	98,379	138,813	41.1	102,447	145,153	41.6
Teachers	4,419	6,099	38.0	3,023	3,552	17.5
Pupils per teacher[42]	37.8	36.3		63.5	67.2	
Average monthly salaries of teachers	$31.64	$41.49	$9.85[43]	$19.39	$20.31	$0.92[43]

[40] United States Commissioner's Report, school age, five to eighteen. Statistics for 1886, school age, five to twenty-one.
[41] United States Commissioner's Report.
[42] On the basis of number of pupils enrolled.
[43] Aggregate; minus sign means decrease.

CHAPTER VII

THE STATUS OF THE TEACHING BODY

Period Between 1886 and 1900. The state superintendent in his Reports in 1891–1893 and 1893–1895 showed that the plan of distributing the state school fund, prescribed in the constitution of 1890, had worked to the advantage of the 'black counties'. Did this advantage result in better school facilities for the large number of Negroes resident in these counties? Did it result in poorer facilities for the Negroes resident in the 'white counties'?

The state distribution could not be used for school buildings, or for repairs, or for furniture. Nor could it be used to increase the length of term in one district of a county without increasing the length of terms in all districts. To this extent, then, white and colored children shared equally the advantage derived by the favored counties. It is true that when the schools of a county could be supported entirely from the state distribution, the people were free to apply their local revenues toward increasing the efficiency of their schools in other ways. But the state distribution went chiefly to pay the salaries of teachers.

In order to determine the extent to which the unequal distribution affected the status of the teaching profession in various parts of the state, I have continued the comparative study made by the superintendent in 1893–1895. The code of 1892 [1] prescribed the following schedule of salaries for teachers in the public schools:

> Third grade, $15 to $20
> Second grade, $18 to $30
> First grade, $25 to $55

The law added: "In fixing the salary the superintendent must take into consideration the executive and teaching capacity of the teachers, and the size of the school, to be determined both by the educable population of the district and the average attendance of the preceding year."

[1] Annotated Code of 1892, Section 2026.

TABLE V

COMPARATIVE SALARIES OF TEACHERS, 1892–1893

Ten White Counties (City and Country Schools)

COUNTY	TOTAL SALARIES		AVERAGE MONTHLY SALARIES	
	White	Colored	White	Colored
Alcorn	$8,506	$2,621	$31.04	$20.85
Calhoun	8,510	2,452	22.99	15.67
Choctaw	5,375	2,072	26.35	22.53
Covington	4,174	1,381	23.46	21.39
Itawamba	9,681	1,083	21.25	19.70
Jones	4,273	659	14.65	16.86
Leake	6,998	2,273	26.20	18.60
Marion	5,644	1,182	28.67	17.08
Pontotoc	10,091	2,199	27.92	18.06
Smith	5,889	939	21.41	14.20
Total	$69,141	$16,861	$24.39	$18.49

Ten Black Counties

COUNTY	TOTAL SALARIES		AVERAGE MONTHLY SALARIES	
	White	Colored	White	Colored
Bolivar	$8,725	$11,526	$49.45	$28.33
Claiborne	10,240	7,957	36.90	26.76
Coahoma	6,134	4,565	42.59	19.50
De Soto	8,722	6,019	39.06	24.61
Holmes	10,941	9,310	40.48	24.25
Issaquena	1,965	3,124	53.50	26.30
Le Flore	4,950	5,284	48.00	21.81
Lowndes	13,818	7,325	44.72	22.06
Monroe	15,330	7,181	35.57	16.94
Washington	12,116	16,155	51.32	29.70
Total	$92,941	$78,446	$44.15	$24.02

The law gave freedom for a considerable amount of variability in respect to salary. Let us see how the plan worked out. The state superintendent's study called attention to the unduly large amounts which the black counties received through the state distribution. Table V shows how these amounts were applied to the salaries of teachers. We may conclude from this table that:

1. The black counties were paying, in the aggregate, very much larger amounts to teachers than were being paid in the white counties.

2. The average salary of Negro teachers in both white and black counties was considerably lower than the average salary of white teachers.

3. Negro teachers in the black counties were almost as well provided for as white teachers in the sparsely settled counties. In fact, four black counties were paying Negro teachers salaries in excess of the average salary of white teachers in the ten white counties.

On the basis of these conclusions, are we to surmise that the black counties were employing in their schools teachers with a higher grade of certificate than the white counties were able to employ? Or, were they paying teachers of similar qualifications to those in the white counties, salaries nearer the maximum figures in the graded schedule?

Table VI throws light on this query. It is perfectly evident from this table that first-grade teachers in the white schools of both white and black counties outnumbered the second and third-grade teachers. Further, it is evident that third-grade teachers predominate in Negro schools of both white and black counties. Table VII gives this information in terms of percentages. From these data we may conclude, that:

1. The average Negro teacher in the black counties, although he received a larger salary than his co-laborer in the white counties, was not so well qualified for his position—so far as a certificate indicates ability to teach.

2. The higher salary of the Negro teachers in the black counties was not due to their holding higher grades of certificate, but to the fact that their salaries were fixed nearer the upper margin of the graded schedule. For instance, third-grade teachers in the black counties, instead of receiving $15, possibly received salaries near $20, the legal maximum to which a third-grade teacher was entitled.

TABLE VI

NUMBER OF TEACHERS OF EACH GRADE, 1892–1893

Ten White Counties

COUNTY	WHITE			COLORED		
	First	Second	Third	First	Second	Third
Alcorn	29	17	7	3	2	18
Calhoun	65	11	0	7	13	10
Choctaw	47	4	0	12	10	1
Covington	47	1	1	8	5	3
Itawamba	49	35	0	1	9	1
Jones	35	25	1	1	3	6
Leake	37	18	6	3	14	12
Marion	56	4	0	3	5	10
Pontotoc	38	31	2	1	10	14
Smith	63	15	1	1	8	6
Total	466	161	18	40	79	81

Ten Black Counties

COUNTY	WHITE			COLORED		
	First	Second	Third	First	Second	Third
Bolivar	34	2	0	24	35	33
Claiborne	18	18	0	6	28	9
Coahoma	25	3	0	7	6	45
De Soto	41	7	0	11	11	31
Holmes	58	2	0	22	44	19
Issaquena	9	0	0	12	9	12
Le Flore	19	1	0	18	21	27
Lowndes	41	9	4	1	18	45
Monroe	49	35	4	2	9	76
Washington	32	0	0	14	44	51
Total	326	77	8	117	225	348

TABLE VII

PER CENT. OF TEACHERS OF EACH GRADE IN WHITE AND
BLACK COUNTIES, 1892–1893

RACE	WHITE COUNTIES			BLACK COUNTIES		
	First	*Second*	*Third*	*First*	*Second*	*Third*
White teachers	72.2	24.9	2.5	79.3	18.7	1.9
Colored teachers	20.0	39.5	40.5	16.9	32.6	50.4

Thus we see that the black counties were to some extent sharing their abundance between both white and colored teachers.

3. In general, we may say that higher average salaries for white teachers in all parts of the state were due to the fact that they held higher grades of certificate.

Was there any discrimination on the part of county superintendents against Negro teachers? Was there any disposition on their part to exercise their legal prerogative and fix the salaries of Negro teachers lower than those of white teachers, observing, of course, the legal limits? Was there any disposition on the part of county boards of examiners to keep down the salaries of Negro teachers by granting them lower grades of certificate? We have no data for answering these questions. If the practice of fixing the salaries of Negro teachers lower than those of white teachers was at all general, there was possibly a justification for this. A county superintendent speaking before the State Teachers' Association as early as 1887, gave a reasonable defense of the flexible salary schedule:[2]

Teachers differ immensely in degrees of competency, social standing, and success. Now equitable dealing requires that such differences should be recognized; and, accordingly, the state when fixing her salaries should make it possible to discriminate with due regard to them. It does not follow that all teachers of the same grade should receive the same pay. I believe that a large proportion of our teachers can by rigid economy live upon the salaries as now fixed; and when the general poverty of our people and the respective

[2] Proceedings, State Teachers' Association, 1887.

claims of their teachers are considered, it may be assumed that this ability to live by the salary is the measure of equity. For this proportion, then, I would say that the remuneration is just and adequate.

We may readily see how the principle here advocated applies in Negro schools. Negro teachers, with a lower standard of living, with fewer social wants, and with lower qualifications, did not deserve as high salaries as were paid white teachers.

The fact that there was such a large percentage of the colored teachers who received third-grade certificates gives rise to the query whether Negro teachers were getting as high certificates as they deserved. A negative answer to this question impugns the integrity of the examining boards in almost every county. In the absence of data it would be folly to press such a claim. On the other hand, the low grade of work done in the public schools, and the total lack of high schools for Negroes, leads us to the conclusion that the preparation of Negro teachers could not have been very thorough.

In this connection it would be well to ascertain what the standards of certification were. Very few changes were made in the school law from 1886 to 1896. The Annotated Code of 1892 indicates that a slight change had been made in the list of subjects prescribed for examination.[3] Second- and third-grade applicants were required to stand examination in primary physiology (with special reference to narcotics), in addition to the list of subjects prescribed for second-grade applicants in 1886. The passing mark for a third-grade certificate was set at sixty, for a second-grade certificate, at seventy-five per cent. To the list of subjects required for a first-grade certificate in 1886 were added the history of Mississippi, elements of natural philosophy, civil government, elements of physiology and hygiene (with special reference to narcotics).

Normals and institutes doubtless increased somewhat the efficiency of both white and colored teachers. The benefit of the Peabody Fund had been lost in 1884, and was not restored until 1892. County superintendents, however, were required by the law of 1886 to spend three Saturdays of each month conducting teachers' institutes. This plan was very ineffective and was succeeded in 1892 by what is known as the county institute, conducted for a period of five days each scholastic year.[4] Separate institutes were

[3] *cf.* Laws of 1886, Chap. XXIV, Sections 49 to 53 with Code of 1892, Section 4022.
[4] Report of Superintendent, 1891–1893, p. 15.

held for each race. These were infinitely better than the old plan, but by 1899 they had "outgrown their usefulness,"[5] and the superintendent recommended that several counties combine and conduct a normal for a longer period.

In the year in which the state was restored to the benefit of the Peabody Fund a colored normal was opened at Holly Springs and another at Tougaloo.[6] In 1895 two additional colored normals were opened for teachers in other parts of the state. Competent white instructors were employed in these normals. The course of study covered four weeks. By 1899 there were eleven Peabody normals running in the state, six of which were for colored teachers. They received from the fund $2,800, from the state, $2,500, and a local supplement from the towns in which the normals were held.[7] In 1897 there were 1801 white and 610 Negro teachers trained in these schools.

By 1897 the normals and county institutes had been worked into a system.[8] First, a conductor's institute was held for two weeks at some central location where thirty-six picked men were trained to conduct county institutes; second, the Peabody summer schools were conducted by the same men who trained the conductors; third, the county institutes were conducted by pairs of men trained in the conductor's school. Two institutes were conducted in the county at the same time, one for each race.

Superintendent Preston seems to have been interested in improving the standards of colored teachers. In his report (1894) of the Negro normals to the Peabody trustees, he said:[9]

The colored race was amply provided for this year. All the instructors were white. The Negroes themselves prefer competent white instructors. I selected the instructors with great care, choosing only such as were capable and of the proper spirit—men who believe in educating the Negro race, and are willing to help them in their efforts. The Negroes of Mississippi are making good progress. Under our strict uniform examinations, 596 make first-grade licenses. There is no end to the persistency with which they seek to better their qualifications . . . In one county I found seventeen colored teachers in a county institute, and all but one had been to college. . .

[5] Report of Superintendent, 1898–1899, p. 27.
[6] Proceedings, Peabody Fund Trustees, Vol. V, pp. 33, 91.
[7] Report of Superintendent, 1898–1899.
[8] Proceedings, Peabody Fund Trustees, Vol. V, p. 278.
[9] *Ibid.*, p. 91.

They teach in the winter and attend college in the summer. Their persistency deserves commendation, and is bound to result in good progress.

The state institutions were in the meantime contributing their share toward the education of the Negro. State support for the Normal Department at Tougaloo, however, was withdrawn by constitutional prescription in 1890. Up to this time its work seems to have been very creditable.[10]

The attendance at the State Normal College at Holly Springs rose from 162 in 1890 to nearly 200 in 1900. From 1877 to 1890 the annual state appropriation had been $3,000. In 1890, however, the appropriation was cut to $2,500. A two years' course was offered. The catalog of 1890 outlines the course of study as follows:[11]

FIRST YEAR

First Term. Rhetorical reading; history, United States; arithmetic, written and mental; geography, political and physical; algebra, introductory; grammar; written spelling; writing and drawing.

Second Term. Rhetoric and composition; civil government; physiology, natural philosophy; algebra; geometry, introductory; drawing.

SECOND YEAR

First Term. Geometry, plane and solid; trigonometry, plane; history, universal; natural history, zoology; chemistry; theory and practice of teaching.

Second Term. Surveying and navigation; geology; botany; mental and moral philosophy; English literature; theory and practice of teaching.

Practice teaching for the older pupils was provided by the organization of a model class from the junior students. Vocal and instrumental music were offered. An excerpt from the report of the president to the State Department indicates the character of the course of study offered in the later nineties:[12]

The literary course is broad and thorough, so a normal student has a good knowledge of English, United States history, the natural sciences, and mathematics; and theory and practice of teaching, history of education, reforms of eminent teachers, psychology, and a short course in Latin.

---

[10] Message of Governor Stone, 1892; 1894.
[11] Mayes: *History of Education in Mississippi*, p. 266. Gives an account of this institution up to 1890.
[12] Report of Superintendent, 1895–1897.

Governor Lowry in 1884 had characterized Alcorn Agricultural and Mechanical College as practically a normal shool for the colored race, since so large a proportion of its students went into teaching.[13] It is probably true that a large number of its graduates continued to become teachers. In 1890 there were seven members of the faculty and two hundred and forty-five students. Up to that date, however, there had been only forty-six graduates. Courses were then offered in mental and moral philosophy, English literature, bookkeeping, political economy, and music, in addition to the sciences and the industrial subjects.[14]

From 1894 to 1898, internal dissensions which called for legislative interference, decreased the efficiency of the institution. The president was dismissed, a new man was installed who was out of harmony with the faculty, and friction continued.[15] In spite of these troubles the enrolment reached 390 in 1897. An able board of trustees in 1896 projected a thorough reorganization of the school, and recommended larger appropriations for the development of the industrial department. The report of the executive committee [16] states the purpose of the reorganization in the following terms:

> We are of the opinion that the Negroes can be best aided by making them skilled laborers in every line of industry. To do this we must have better equipment, and for that purpose especially we make an earnest plea for an increased appropriation.

Governor McLaurin stated in 1900 that affairs at Alcorn were now harmonious and that the institution was a "credit to the colored race."[17]

With the summer normals, the county institutes, and the state institutions directing their efforts toward the development of the teaching profession, good results were forthcoming. The state superintendent in 1895 stated [18] that in ten years the number of first-grade colored teachers rose from 238 to 600, so that at that date more than twenty per cent. of those employed in colored schools held first-grade certificates. By 1901 the number of first-grade

[13] Senate Journal, 1884, p. 27, Governor's Message.
[14] Mayes: *History of Education in Mississippi*, p. 270.
[15] Senate Journal, 1894, p. 21; 1898, p. 171.
[16] Report of Superintendent, 1895–1897, p. 261.
[17] House Journal, 1900, p. 12, Governor's Message.
[18] Report of Superintendent, 1893–1895, p. 36.

teachers had risen to 675, representing an increase of a little more than one per cent. in six years; so, while we may say that there had been progress, the advance was rather slow.

The Status of the Teaching Body, 1900–1910. The report of the state superintendent in 1903 asserted that ninety per cent. of the teachers of Mississippi were not professionally trained, and that seventy-five per cent. had never attended any school other than the rural school.[19] The only professional training received by the white teachers of the state was that provided by the summer normals, the county institutes and the departments of pedagogy in the state institutions. The work done in the summer normals consisted simply of a review of the common branches, and the study of a "standard text-book on pedagogy." They were conducted by skilled teachers who were supposed to emphasize the practical side of the work.[20]

In 1899 eleven white normals of one month each were held. Colored normals were held at Greenville, Vicksburg, New Albany, Okolona, Macon, and Newton. The normal at Vicksburg was this year conducted by five capable white men. Courses were pursued in grammar, literature, rhetoric, physics, physiology, first-year Latin, arithmetic, geometry, civil government, and pedagogy. The director of this normal recommended that Latin be not attempted again in so short a term. The representative Negro teachers of the state were present at this normal, and they organized a State Teachers' Association for Negroes.[21]

The results accomplished in the county institutes were disappointing. They were too short to make possible a review of the common branches and at the same time to arouse interest and enthusiasm in educational endeavor.[22] The salaries paid rural teachers were so small that they did not feel justified in attending. Yet the State Department thought the training which they offered was infinitely better than none.

An elaborate outline of studies to be pursued in the normals was issued from the state office in 1901.[23] It contained outlines of the

---

[19] Report of Superintendent, 1901–1903, p. 8.
[20] *Ibid.*, 1897–1899, p. 2.
[21] *Ibid.*, 1897–1899, p. 2.
[22] *Ibid.*, p. 27.
[23] *Ibid.*, 1899–1901, p. 159.

following subjects: psychology, school management, practical elements in the art of teaching, elementary work (including the regular school subjects), nature study, literature, story-telling, drawing, physical culture, singing, German, geography, United States history, Mississippi history, civil government, written and mental arithmetic, physics, and physiology. The wide range of studies here offered does not indicate, of course, that all these subjects were taught in all the schools.

The need of a state normal school for white teachers had been repeatedly pointed out ever since the establishment of the public school system. The legislature, however, could never be induced to establish such a school. It was only in 1911 that a bill establishing such a school was finally approved.

In 1901, Holly Springs State Normal School had a building, originally worth $12,000. The equipment was by no means adequate to accommodate the number of students that could be obtained. Between two and three hundred students were in attendance. Three years of preparatory work were offered in addition to the two years' normal course. The president claimed that the curriculum was "equal to that of an ordinary college course," but it surely did not go far beyond the secondary subjects.[24] The foreign languages had been abandoned, and emphasis was now being laid on psychology, educational theory, and methods. The school ceased to exist in 1904 when the legislature refused to vote an appropriation for its support. Since 1904 the only normal training provided for Negroes has been at Alcorn, in the private institutions, and in the normals and institutes. Up until 1901 there had been nearly two hundred graduates from the State Normal School, and the president had never heard of one who had been convicted of a serious crime.

Alcorn, in 1907, was accommodating over five hundred students, and the attendance was limited to the number that could be lodged.[25] "Several hundred" were being turned away. Many of the students were mature men and women who had found it embarrassing to continue longer in the public schools. A nine-year course was provided, which permitted students to enter from the fourth grade. The five-year preparatory course was also called a normal course. Not over twenty-five per cent. of those who completed this depart-

[24] Report of Superintendent, 1899–1901, p. 24.
[25] *Ibid.*, 1905–1907, p. 12.

ment entered the college. In 1906, sixteen graduated from the scientific department of the college, sixty-five from the preparatory (normal) department, and fifteen from the industrial departments. It is clear that Alcorn was making a considerable contribution to the teaching profession, in spite of the fact that the institution was supposed to emphasize the agricultural course.

Having now considered the advantages of normal training offered to the teaching body in Mississippi, let us pass to a consideration of its standing from the point of view of qualifications as represented in the grade of certificate issued. Few, if any, changes had been made since 1892 in the requirements for the different grades of certificate. After 1896, doubtless the requirement that the State Board of Examiners examine the papers of applicants for state license, tended to lift the standard of efficiency of the teaching body.

From the statistical tables indicating the number of teachers of each race and grade, found in the Reports of the State Superintendent, the author has computed the following percentages:

GRADE	1889–1890		1900–1901[26]		1909–1910	
	White	*Colored*	*White*	*Colored*	*White*	*Colored*
First grade	61.7	14.2	83.7	21.4	91.4	23.6
Second grade	33.5	45.9	14.0	39.3	7.8	24.7
Third grade	4.9	39.8	1.9	39.1	1.4	51.6

So far as the status of the Negro teachers of Mississippi is concerned, there is but one conclusion to be reached. Their efficiency, as represented by the grade of certificate which they held, indicates a slight improvement during the eleven years between 1890 and 1901, and a very decided retrogression during the nine years between 1901 and 1910. We may account for this falling back in a number of ways. The closing of the Holly Springs Normal School undoubtedly accounts for a part of it. The Negro schools in many parts of the state were undoubtedly demoralized by the unfavorable trend of public opinion, and were able less easily to turn out efficient teachers.

[26] Statistics for 1899–1900 were not summarized in the report for this year.

If demoralization is reflected in the grade of certificate which the teachers were using, it is no less reflected in the salaries which they were earning. In 1898, the salaries of white teachers ranged from $16.00 in Perry and $19.19 in Jones, to $44.20 in Coahoma and $42 in Sharkey.[27] Salaries of Negro teachers for the same year ranged from $11.54 in Clarke and $12.86 in Grenada, to $26.68 in Sharkey and $26 in Sunflower. While these averages were probably inaccurate in some instances, they indicate fairly well that there was a wide difference between the amounts paid teachers in one part of the state, and the amounts paid teachers in other parts of the state; they indicate also that there was a wide difference between the amounts paid Negro teachers and the amounts paid white teachers; they indicate, further, that many teachers, white and colored, were receiving a bare living wage, if so much.

The table indicating the average salaries paid teachers from year to year (Statistical Summary, p. 141), shows that the average salary of white teachers in the rural schools rose from a general average for the entire state in 1901, of $30.64 to $42.38 in 1910; it shows that during the same interval the average salary for Negro teachers rose from $19.39 to $20.52. Such an advance in the salaries of white teachers has not a parallel in any other decade of the history of the schools. Undoubtedly there had been a tremendous awakening to the need of education in the state. That the Negro schools did not to any appreciable extent share the benefits of this awakening, is clearly evident from these figures. If Negro teachers deserved no better salaries than these, they certainly represented a very low degree of efficiency.

In conclusion, the very best picture of the teaching profession in the schools for Negroes, is not a bright one. If the tendency has not been positively backward, it has certainly not been forward. Having lost the Normal Department in Tougaloo by constitutional prescription in 1890, and having lost the State Normal School at Holly Springs in 1904 by failure of the legislature to appropriate funds for its support, the Negroes have left them as the only institution for training teachers, an institution primarily designed for agricultural and industrial instruction. It can hardly be hoped that the meager training furnished by the public schools will provide more efficient teachers than those which now man the schools.

[27] Report of Superintendent, 1897–1899, Statistics.

CHAPTER VIII

THE DISTRIBUTION OF THE COMMON SCHOOL FUND

Period Between 1886 and 1900. The common school fund up to 1890 had been distributed to the counties in proportion to the number of educable children. The poll tax, however, had not been included in the common school fund. The new Constitution made a change in the wording of the section on this subject, which very vitally affected Negro education. For the sake of clearness it will be well to quote the section as it was adopted by the Convention of 1890:[1]

There shall be a common school fund which shall consist of the poll tax (to be retained in the counties where the same is collected) and an additional sum from the general fund of the state treasury, which together shall be sufficient to maintain the common schools for the term of four months in each scholastic year. But any county or separate school district may levy an additional tax to maintain its schools for a longer time than four months. The common school fund shall be distributed among the several counties and separate districts in proportion to the number of educable children in each, to be determined from data collected through the office of the State Superintendent of Education, in the manner to be prescribed by law.

At first sight it might appear that such a law would furnish an equitable distribution of the school fund, since it requires the rich and prosperous sections of the state to lend support to the schools in the less prosperous sections. In Mississippi conditions have been such as to make the plan prove a very inequitable means of distribution.

The situation was complicated by the unequal distribution of the population. In the sparsely settled poor counties the white race predominated. The Negro population of the state in 1890 was 742,559; of this number 401,639 were concentrated in twenty-three counties, in the ratio of 362 to every 100 whites.[2] In addition,

---

[1] Constitution of 1890, Section 206.
[2] United States Commissioner's Report, 1900–1901, Kelly Miller: *The Education of the Negro*, p. 741.

191,420 Negroes inhabited sixteen other counties, in the ratio of 130 to every 100 whites. This accounts for 593,059 out of the 742,559, or nearly eighty per cent., which portion of the population was made up largely of tenants on the rich Delta and prairie lands of the state, outnumbering the whites in certain counties more than eight to one. Thus the section of the state on which the commonwealth might rely to defray a part of the expense of maintaining schools in the sparsely settled counties, was itself burdened with a large non-tax-paying population.

It was very important that the state school fund be equitably distributed since the schools at this time were drawing a large part of their support from this fund. The superintendent in 1895 declared that seventy-four and one-half per cent. of all school funds was provided by the poll tax and the state distribution, and that only about fourteen per cent. was coming from local taxation.[3] The expenditures for all educational purposes in 1892–1893 amounted to $1,321,012, or the equivalent of 7.1 mills on the total assessed valuation of all property.[4] For this year Mississippi led all southern states in this particular, and stood eighth among the states of the Union. Mississippi was thus going to an extreme in levying a state tax, and was neglecting to encourage the local units to help themselves. The general practice of the majority of the states was to levy a small state tax and thus force the local units to make heavy levies for their schools. In most states the general tax did not exceed eighteen per cent. From the facts that have preceded it may readily be inferred that an equitable distribution of the state school fund was very important.

The wording of Section 206 was of doubtful meaning. It is hard to tell whether the framers of the section intended that the poll tax should be left in the counties, and only the state fund distributed according to the number of educable children, or whether the poll tax was to be combined with the state fund and the whole sum disbursed in this way. At any rate, the second interpretation was accepted, and the poll tax, although retained in the counties, was considered a part of the state distribution. While the first interpretation unquestionably meant a more equitable distribution of the school fund among the tax-payers, it made the distribution less

[3] Report of Superintendent, 1893–1895, p. 24.
[4] *Ibid.*, 1891–1893, p. 4.

equitable for the children, white and colored. The interpretation which was accepted therefore worked to the advantage of the Negro schools—at least to the advantage of the counties in which the colored race was dominant. This we shall understand presently.

The year 1892–1893 was marked by a slump of 7,527 in the enrolment of the whites in the public schools,[5] and by an increase of 1,523 in the enrolment of Negroes. The figures for average attendance showed a similar tendency. First-grade white teachers decreased 361, and first-grade Negro teachers decreased 77; 119 white and 96 colored schools were closed; 338 fewer white teachers, and 87 fewer colored teachers were employed this year than the year before; white salaries decreased $45,275 and Negro salaries, $20,341. The whites showed a decrease in all items, while the Negroes showed marked gains in some instances.

The superintendent assigned as the reason for the slump the unjust workings of Section 206 which had just gone into effect, but, since the figures for the next year indicate a return almost to normal enrolment, attendance, etc., it is doubtful if this cause operated to the extent he feared. Nevertheless, Mr. Preston's statistical investigation of the inequality of the means of distribution is of interest just here.

He pointed out that in Washington and Bolivar Counties, where the Negroes outnumbered the whites more than eight to one, the schools were run seven and five months respectively; whereas, in Jones and Smith, where the whites outnumbered the blacks five to one, Jones had had a term of sixty-five days, and Smith a term of seventy-seven, or considerably less than four months each. The average salary of teachers in the two Delta counties had been about $37.00, and in the two white counties, about $16.00. By way of summary, he said:[6]

In many of the white counties, where the population is sparse, salaries are so meager that teachers cannot be employed, and the schools of many districts are not taught at all, while in others, the patrons are compelled to supplement the salary paid by the county.

In the biennial reports both for 1891–1893 and for 1893–1895, the statistical studies which attempted to prove the inequality of the means of distribution are very interesting. The chief point

[5] Report of Superintendent, 1891–1893, p. 1.
[6] *Ibid.*, p. 2.

attacked was the inequality caused by considering the poll tax collected in each county as a part of the state distribution. The superintendent compared statistical data collected from ten 'black counties' with data collected from ten 'white counties'. He showed that, according to the current plan, the white counties of the state received more from the school fund than they paid into it; that a large part of the tax which they paid consisted of the tax on white polls; further, that the black counties paid fewer poll taxes, and, in proportion to their wealth, contributed little toward the support of schools in other counties.

Certain conclusions which the superintendent drew, aside from proving the inequality of the means of distribution, throw light upon school conditions of that day. It will be well to quote them in full:

The white counties have 744 schools, for the support of which they receive from the state distribution $89,463, or $120 for each school. The mean average term of schools in these counties is 89 days for the country schools, and the average salary per month for teachers of both races is $21.76. The average salary in nine of these counties is less than $22, and in Pontotoc $25.13, which is the highest.

The black counties have 882 schools; they receive for each $190; have a term of 111 days, and pay in country schools an average salary of $29.95—the highest being $34 in Bolivar.

The black counties have 40 per cent. longer terms and pay 37 per cent. better salaries, but they enrolled 64 pupils to each school while the white counties enrolled 52 pupils.

In the ten black counties the white teachers numbered 445 and were paid in salaries $101,320, or $288 apiece; while the colored teachers numbered 725 and were paid $80,952, or $112 apiece.

It thus appears that the main advantage gained by the black counties accrues to the white children thereof.

There are three factors that make it cheaper to maintain schools in the black counties, *viz.*, fewer first-grade teachers, larger schools to the teacher, a lower percentage of pupils in average attendance.

In concluding his investigation, the superintendent recommended an amendment to the constitution[7] to remedy the situation. His plan was to cut the amount of the state distribution to a three-months' allowance, and to force the counties to levy for the support of their schools an amount not less than one-fifth of the state appor-

[7] Report of Superintendent, 1893–1895, p. 30.

tionment. From the fund thus raised counties were to be required
to maintain schools for four months. The plan contemplated the
raising of the school fund by a two-dollar poll tax (to be retained
in the counties), by a two-mill *ad valorem* tax, and by setting aside
one-half the state revenues derived from the taxation of railroads.

It seems to have been generally conceded, even by those who
wished the Negro to have every opportunity for education, that
the provision for the distribution of the school fund furnished by
Section 206, was partial and unfair. The superintendent pleaded
with the legislature of 1892 to submit an amendment to the people.
Such an amendment was reported favorably in the House, but failed
to receive the constitutional majority required to pass it.[8] In 1894,
an amendment passed the third reading in the House by a vote of
82 to 19, and was lost in the Senate 20 to 19.[9] In 1896, Governor
Stone recommended an amendment which would require the
counties to assist in the support of the schools. In this he seems to
have concurred with the state superintendent. The same year a
Senate Concurrent Resolution to amend Section 206 so as to impose
an *ad valorem* tax of two mills, passed the Senate by a vote of
33 to 11, but was lost in the House by 51 to 46.[10] An unsuccessful
attempt was made in the Senate to amend the measure just mentioned, so as to provide for the division of the school funds between
the races in proportion to the amount of taxes paid by each. In
1900 four bills were before the Senate offering to amend the section.
One was indefinitely postponed; one failed to pass; one was withdrawn; one never came to a vote.[11] Attempts to amend the section have been made during almost every succeeding session of the
legislature.

From the above survey it is clear that the legislature would have
adopted a different plan of distribution if a plurality vote could
have secured an amendment to the constitution. The texts of the
various amendments which were proposed have never been published, so we have no means of determining to what extent these suggestions would have affected the education of the Negro. We know,
however, that the suggestion to divide the school fund, placed before

[8] House Journal, 1892, p. 804.
[9] Senate Journal, 1894, p. 253.
[10] *Ibid.*, 1896, S. C. R. Nos. 5 and 11.
[11] *Ibid.*, 1900, p. 730.

the Senate in 1896, would have been a sore discrimination against Negro schools.

Superintendent Preston, after a period of service covering ten strenuous years, was succeeded in 1896 by A. A. Kincannon. Mr. Kincannon shared Mr. Preston's views in regard to the education of the Negro and the inequality of the present means of distribution. His position is defined in the following quotation:[12]

> The evil effects of Section 206 are causing grave unrest with many taxpayers and with many thoughtful citizens of the state. Smarting under the impositions of this section, some have unwisely suggested that this method of apportionment be so modified that the school fund shall be divided between the races according to the tax money paid by each race. To the conservative man this proposition is not only unwise but dangerous. The proposition to divide the school funds according to the taxes paid by the two races of the state, followed to its logical conclusion, means that the poor man shall have only such educational advantages as he provides by taxing himself.

The new superintendent's remedy for the situation was substantially the same as that of his predecessor. He would have the poll tax retained in the counties and supplemented by the state and local levies to an amount sufficient to run the schools at least four months. H. L. Whitfield, who succeeded Mr. Kincannon in office in September, 1898, also held this view.[13]

The Distribution of the Common School Fund (1900–1901). The agitation to secure a more equitable distribution of the school fund, by a substitution or an amendment of Section 206 of the Constitution, reached fever heat about 1900. The press of the state, especially in the white counties, was alive on the subject.[14] State Senator Rowan, who in 1896 had offered a resolution proposing a division of the school fund between the races, waged a newspaper controversy with Major W. H. Gibbs, also a legislator,[15] in which Rowan contended that he was not opposed to the education of the Negro, but to heavy taxes; hence he favored a division of the school funds on the basis of the amount of tax paid by each race. Gibbs replied that it was unjust and very poor politics thus to break up the schools for Negroes, and disturb the harmony existing between the races.

[12] Report of Superintendent, 1898–1899, p. 30.
[13] *Ibid.*, p. 10.
[14] *Clarion Ledger*, December 7, 1899; January 18, 1900.
[15] *Ibid.*, December 14, 16, 1899.

So strong had public sentiment become that Governor Longino felt constrained to forestall radical action on the subject by discussing it in his inaugural address.[16] He said in part:

> There has been some urgent insistence for the submission by this legislature of an amendment to the state Constitution to provide for the distribution of the free school funds between the white and Negro schools of the state, so as to give the benefits thereof to each race in proportion to the school taxes which each pays . . . Its effect, which would be to take school benefits largely from Negro children, would be contrary to that broad philanthropic spirit that has moved the great common heart of Christian man and womanhood of Mississippi to a love of justice and fair play toward the weak and needy. . .

The Governor favored an amendment which would cause the fund to be distributed on the basis of average attendance in the schools.

Five concurrent resolutions, having as their object the amendment of Section 206, were introduced in the House in 1900. One of these proposed to have the school fund divided on the basis of the amount of the tax paid by each race. All were reported adversely either by the Committee on Constitution, or by the Committee on Education.[17] Four similar bills were before the Senate at this session, but only one seems to have come to a vote.

Major Vardaman, candidate for the governorship in 1903, made a campaign issue of the division of the school fund. His position, to state it briefly, was that the money formerly spent on the education of the Negro had been wasted, inasmuch as no improvement could be noted in the moral nature of the Negro.[18] To use Mr. Vardaman's own words, "His civilization veneer lasts just as long as he remains in contact with the white man. Then why squander money on his education when the only effect is to spoil a good field hand and make an insolent cook." He advocated the amendment of Section 206, so as to leave the distribution of the school funds entirely in the hands of the legislature.[19]

The legislature of 1904 wrote into the constitution an amendment [20] to Section 206, which provided for the retention of the poll

---

[16] Senate Journal, 1900, p. 93.
[17] House Journal, 1900, p. 326.
[18] *Times-Democrat*, report of Crystal Springs Chautauqua speech, July 23, 1903.
[19] Inaugural Address, Senate Journal, 1904, p. 123; 1908, p. 10.
[20] Laws of 1904, Chap. 173.

tax in the counties. The framers of the constitution seem to have intended that this tax be kept in the counties and not considered a part of the state distribution, but a faulty wording of Section 206 prevented their intentions from being carried out. Ever since 1895 attempts had been made to rectify the error but a constitutional majority could never be secured in the legislature.

Messrs. Noel and Critz, representing what was known in the newspapers as the conservative element, were defeated for the gubernatorial nomination by Vardaman in 1903. This seemed to give the endorsement of the state to Vardaman's plan for distributing the school fund, but the issue was not pressed. Noel, who was again a candidate in 1907, was elected, and, in his inaugural address, expressed his approval of a plan to distribute the fund on the basis of average attendance.[21] An amendment proposing such a means of distribution was introduced in the House, but was lost along with eight other bills which had in view the amendment of Section 206. The Committee on Constitution reported unfavorably seven such bills in one day.[22] Three such bills got an unfavorable report in the Senate. The bill which gained the largest following in the House during this session was House Concurrent Resolution No. 1, which proposed to create a "county school fund, a state school fund, and a state common school fund." This, however, was finally tabled, and when brought up before the next legislature was defeated by a large majority. An attempt to amend Section 206 was successful enough to reach a vote in the Senate in 1910, but failed to pass.

These successive and persistent attempts to amend Section 206, covering as they have nearly twenty years, indicate widespread discontent with the constitutional method of distributing the school fund. Four governors and three state superintendents were pronounced in their opposition. The legislature, however, seems to have been averse to making a change. The only amendment which was ever made, was a slight change which required that the poll tax should henceforth be retained in the counties, and should not form a part of the state distribution. The prolonged agitation of the question undoubtedly caused public sentiment to be kindled against the education of the Negro.

[21] Senate Journal, 1908, p. 167.
[22] House Journal, 1908, p. 372.

CHAPTER IX

THE CURRICULUM

Period Between 1886 and 1900. The revised school laws of 1886 state that the subjects required for teachers' examinations should constitute the course of study.[1] The law of 1878 with respect to teachers' examinations was modified to some extent. "The higher branches of English literature" and bookkeeping requirements were eliminated, and in their places were substituted English composition, physiology, and mental arithmetic. In this connection it is interesting to note that when the new school law came before the state Senate [2] in 1886 it failed to pass, chiefly because of a clause requiring physiology to be taught with "special reference to the effects of alcoholics upon the human system." Several days later, however, the troublesome clause was pruned out and the bill passed by a good majority.

The school reformers had to wait until 1892 to get the clause with reference to alcoholics incorporated into law.[3] The revision of the law provided for in the Annotated Code of 1892, offered an opportunity not only for this addition but also for the introduction of two other statutory subjects, Mississippi history and civil government.

The teaching of United States history since Reconstruction days had been watched by the lovers of the old South with jealous attention. If the history used in the schools treated the Civil War from the northern point of view, it found instant condemnation. By statute of 1890,[4] the state superintendent, the attorney general, and the governor were named as a committee to examine history texts and to place their approval upon such as were deemed suitable for use in the schools of the state.

Perhaps one of the best means of determining the upper limits of the course of study in Negro schools will be an investigation of the entrance requirements of such institutions as Alcorn and Holly

[1] Laws of 1886, Chap. XXIV, Sections 49–53.
[2] Senate Journal, 1886, pp. 516, 561.
[3] Annotated Code of 1892, 4016–4018.
[4] Laws of 1890, Chap. 74

Springs State Normal. Institutions of this type are forced to place their course within reach of the public schools. In 1888 we find that Alcorn [5] was requiring all applicants for entrance to stand an examination on White's *Intermediate Arithmetic*, Swinton's *Fourth Reader*, Monteith's *Manual of Geography*, and Swinton's *Word-Book*. In other words, fourth- or fifth-grade preparation would secure admittance. For admission to the State Normal, preparation slightly more advanced than this was required. Judging from these facts we may fix the upper limits of public school instruction for Negroes somewhere near the fourth or fifth grade. It is highly probable that only the more "promising lads" got this far.

By 1890 the law requiring uniform texts in each county seems to have been observed with a fair degree of satisfaction. In order to convey an idea of the popularity of certain texts the following figures have been tabulated from the report of the state superintendent: [6]

> Swinton's Word-Book was used in twenty-eight counties.
> McGuffey's Readers in twenty-six.
> Maury's Geography in thirty-three.
> Robinson's Mental Arithmetic in fifty-seven.
> Robinson's Practical Arithmetic in forty-seven.
> Reed and Kellogg's Grammar in thirty-eight.
> Reed and Kellogg's Composition in seventeen.
> Chambers' History in forty-six.
> Steele's Physiology in forty-six.
> Steele's Natural Philosophy in sixty-one.

To one familiar with these text-books the nature of the curriculum is apparent. McGuffey's Readers with their stories with a moral purpose, and Robinson's Arithmetics with their superfluous rules, and problems involving the length of time it would take A, B, and C to do a piece of work—good old-fashioned texts, dog-eared with service since 1870—were still holding their own. Swinton's Word-Book, however, with its "Tough Enough Lesson" and others rivaling it in toughness, was now taking the place of Webster's "old blue-back speller." Coming in with the nineties, the innovation of diagrams in Reed and Kellogg's Grammar captivated teachers on the verge of despair over the inability of pupils to comprehend the abstract formality of old-time grammar. Along with the newer

[5] Report of Superintendent, 1888–1889, p. 392.
[6] *Ibid.*, 1890–1891, p. 457.

texts appeared also Steele's Physiology with its catalog of bones and terrible story of the effect of alcohol upon the tissues of the body. Steele's Natural Philosophy, a forerunner of the recently organized general science course, was generally popular. On the whole, we may say that, although still very formal, there were evidences of improvement in the nature of the curriculum.

It can hardly be gainsaid that arithmetic and grammar dominated the curriculum of this period. Much stress seems to have been placed upon solving complicated problems in percentage, square and cube root, and mensuration. In the Outlines for Institutes and in the uniform examination [7] questions, published in the superintendent's reports, there seems to have been an effort to make the work in arithmetic serve a practical purpose, but it is very doubtful if the instruction deviated far into the practical. The work in mental arithmetic consisted in the solving of problems in the fundamental processes, fractions, profit and loss, discount, and interest, according to a formal 'model analysis'.

Grammar and composition were of a most formal character. Here is a question in the examination on composition in 1886:[8] "Write a composition of ten lines on cotton, using it in a compound, complex, a declarative, an interrogative, and an imperative sentence." Composition as an art seems seldom to have been taught. Instruction in composition consisted of a study of style, figures of speech, and the forms of discourse. It must be admitted, however, that some attention was paid to letter writing—just how much, it is hard to say. In grammar, parsing and diagraming, leading to familiarity with the parts of speech and with syntax, furnished the basis of the course.

In the teaching of geography, the Outlines for Institutes indicate commendable progress in method. Under the heading, "Things to be Avoided in Studying Geography" the Outlines list the following:

a. Memorizing the text-books.

b. Giving too much time to things of little importance to the pupil.

c. Failure to give due attention to those places and things of prime importance; such as: 1. Great commercial and manufacturing centers. 2. Places of historical importance. 3. Rivers valuable to commerce. 4. Mountain ranges and ocean currents, as modifying the climate and commerce of countries.

[7] Report of Superintendent, 1886–1887.
[8] *Ibid.*, 1886–1887, Outlines for Institutes; examination questions.

It was also suggested that the pupil be made thoroughly familiar with the geography of his state and community. It must be remembered, however, that the Outlines represent the most advanced theory, and that possibly only the best teachers in the most progressive communities even attempted to put them into practice.

The social and civic value of United States history seems scarcely to have been comprehended. The introduction of civil government in 1892, however, indicates that there was a conscious striving toward the ideal of good citizenship.

As early as 1886 teachers were interested in the discussion of the relative merits of the phonic, word and alphabetic methods of teaching reading. The Outlines suggest that some attention be paid to silent reading. Under the lax system of supervision in the rural schools it is doubtful if new theories gained very wide acceptance. The alphabetic method was certainly in use until quite recently.

From the Outlines for Institutes, from the examination questions, and from the texts that were used, we get but an imperfect idea of what was actually done in the schools. If white rural communities have been backward and loath to exchange old-fashioned ideas and practices for new, we may be sure that the Negro communities with no supervision, and with little light to illuminate a new pathway, have been even more inclined to remain in the ruts. Formal instruction in reading, writing, arithmetic, and spelling, with possibly a smattering of United States history, geography and physiology, represents about what the Negro schools had to offer the colored youth of Mississippi.

The Curriculum from 1900 to 1910. The opening of the new century found the curriculum still formal, and directed chiefly toward a disciplinary end. Arithmetic and grammar were still at the head. The Outlines for Institutes which appeared in 1901 [9] stated the aim of arithmetic as follows: "The cultivation of the power to reason and the formation of the habit of accurate and rapid calculation are the two great motives in the teaching of arithmetic." Of the aim of grammar the Outlines said: "The primary purpose of the study of grammar is the excellent mental discipline its study furnishes; of the secondary purposes, the acquirement of knowledge for the basis of other language teaching is the more important,

[9] Report of Superintendent, 1900–1901, pp. 166, 173.

while least important of all is the acquirement of knowledge for guidance in speaking and writing." These statements indicate the formal character of the instruction of the day.

But the leaven of progress was at work. A decided tendency toward the enrichment of the program of studies is discernible in the same pages which voice the foregoing disciplinary ideals. Nature study, story-telling, singing, physical culture, busy work in clay, drawing, cutting and folding paper, make their appearance in the Outlines. It is probable, however, that these subjects were incidental and that they claimed little of the time heretofore devoted to the formal subjects. Surely they were not taught in all schools; more likely they found their way but slowly into even the best schools. We may observe in this connection that the principle of correlation was accepted, particularly in the case of geography, nature study, reading, language, spelling, and history.

There began to develop at this time a deepening consciousness that the schools were designed to serve the immediate needs of the people. The recognition of the fact that the problem of education in Mississippi is mainly the problem of making the rural masses socially efficient, was gaining headway. A committee of five, appointed in 1901 by the State Teachers' Association,[10] reported in 1903 a very elaborate and revolutionary plan for the reorganization of education. The report, which is perhaps the most important educational document in the recent history of the state, attacked the traditional curriculum because of its failure to function in the lives of the people. At least four important changes were recommended.

1. That the amount of time and attention devoted to arithmetic should be reduced by eliminating the distinction between 'practical' and 'mental' arithmetic and by consolidating the two separate subjects into one. By applying the knife to the old text and eliminating involution, evolution, allegation, progressions, permutations, foreign exchange, etc., the committee hoped to do away with much useless matter, and to save much time for practical study.

2. That the study of composition should be made more practical. It was freely acknowledged that grammar had failed to function in conversation and writing, and that formal instruction in composition, such as had heretofore been given, had accomplished little.

[10] Report of Superintendent, 1901–1903, p. 82.

The committee recommended that language lessons be introduced into the elementary course, and that more attention be devoted to the art of speaking and writing.

3. That sight-singing, free-hand drawing, and manual training be introduced wherever possible. Attention to these subjects, however, was not stressed by the committee.

4. That natural philosophy be dropped from the list of statutory subjects and that the elements of agriculture be inserted in its place. This is perhaps the most important change that was suggested. By way of explaining its attitude toward this subject, the report says:

> It is evident that the course of study in this state needs readjustment in order to bring it into touch with its surroundings and in order to adapt it to the needs of rural life. Mississippi is predominantly an agricultural state and must always remain so, as her only natural resource is found in her soil. The prosperity of the state is directly dependent upon the development of her agricultural interests. The education of the country boy and girl should awaken an intelligent interest in the things immediately about them. . . It should make evident to them that a trained intelligence brought to bear upon the problems of farm life is a necessity for the highest success. The child should be taught to appreciate the beauty and independence of country life and be satisfied with it.

This final suggestion of the committee met with a favorable reception and we find it incorporated into law in the Annotated Code of 1906.[11] Dating from this report there has been an ever-increasing tendency toward the adaptation of the curriculum to meet the needs of the people. This tendency is perhaps not so evident in changes in the course of study as it is in the methods employed, in the broadening range of school activities, and in the general spirit of the school. The organization of corn clubs among school boys received a substantial backing when in 1908 the county supervisors were authorized by law [12] to appropriate fifty dollars in prizes to the work. Sanitation and hygiene were in the meantime being promoted by the efforts of a field agent of the School Improvement Association.[13]

To what extent did the progressive spirit of the new century enter into the Negro schools? We may be sure that the statutory

[11] Annotated Code of 1906, 4543.
[12] Laws of 1908, Chap. 104.
[13] Report of Superintendent, 1909–1911, p. 8.

subjects were introduced into the schools, but whether they were capably taught is another matter. The state supervisor of rural schools in 1911 reported that [14] fully seventy-five per cent. of all rural schools were one-teacher schools, in which the teachers were required to hear on an average of thirty recitations a day. In the crowded Negro schools we may easily infer that conditions were not at all favorable for instruction. Agriculture, hygiene, and language study, the subjects most needed by the Negroes, must have been poorly taught at best. Besides, since these subjects are usually taught in the upper grades, and very few pupils remained long in school, few received instruction in them. Corn club activities, and activities such as were conducted by the School Improvement Association, only in rare instances, if ever, were allied with Negro schools.

Elsewhere in this treatise I have quoted statements [15] which indicate the position of Senator Vardaman with reference to the curriculum of the Negro schools. He expressed the opinion that literary education had in no way improved the character of the Negro, and suggested that the state revise its plan and "educate his heart and his hands, give him, if possible, a moral basis to build upon." [16] He did not suggest, however, the details of a curriculum for attaining this purpose. The only important suggestion that has been offered for a reorganization along these lines is one to be found in the Address of the President of the State Teachers' Association in 1905.[17] It was here proposed to limit the course of study in Negro schools on its intellectual side to the 'three R's', and to provide ample training along industrial and moral lines. The president characterized the attempt to give high school or classical education to the Negro as "giving a stone to him who asks for bread."

These suggestions have not borne fruit. The same curriculum is used in both white and colored schools. The 'three R's' constitute the basis, as they always have, and, because of the fact that Negro children drop out of school early, very few get more than an imperfect knowledge of even these subjects.

[14] Report of Superintendent 1909–1911, p. 8.
[15] See page 110.
[16] House Journal, 1904, p. 840.
[17] Proceedings, State Teachers' Association, 1905, p. 27.

CHAPTER X

PUBLIC SENTIMENT IN REGARD TO THE EDUCATION OF THE NEGRO SINCE 1886

Public Sentiment, 1886 to 1900. The sentiment of the leading citizens of the state, with few exceptions, has always favored giving the Negroes equal opportunities of elementary education. This may be said, so far as the state government is concerned, to have been the dominant sentiment, despite the reservations that must be made with respect to the counties. Yet, it must be admitted that there has also been a strong element of opposition, which seems to have centered on the question of the proper division between the races of the funds for the support of schools. As the public school system increased in favor with the white people, and as its demands became heavier and heavier, this question came more and more prominently into the foreground. Evidences in support of the foregoing generalizations may be found in the reports of the state superintendent, in the legislative journals, in the Proceedings of the State Teachers' Association, and in the public press.

The attitude of Superintendent Preston, to whom is largely due the credit for the organization of the machinery of the school system, was avowedly in favor of Negro education. His report in 1889 contains the following statement:[1]

Confronted and impeded by the illiteracy and poverty of the colored race, in knitting up the sinews of our shattered civilization, we have for nineteen years treated the Negro fairly, nay generously, in the distribution of our scanty school revenues, and have sought to elevate him in morality and intelligence. We cannot afford to be unjust to this illiterate portion of our population; ignorance and its concomitant vices offer only continuous degradation, shiftlessness, and crime.

In 1887, the State Teachers' Association passed a resolution commending the educational progress of the Negro.[2] The subject of Negro education was discussed not only at this meeting but also

[1] Report of Superintendent, 1888–1889, p. 31.
[2] Proceedings, State Teachers' Association, 1887.

at the meetings in 1889 and 1892. The East Mississippi Teachers' Association also discussed the question. The titles of the discussions indicate that the teachers were impressed with the obligation of the white race to maintain colored schools. [3] The need of industrial education for Negroes was voiced in these discussions.

The point of view of the tax-payer was set forth by a county superintendent of one of the Delta counties at the meeting in 1887. "When you ask me," said he, "to discuss the cause of education in the Delta, you ask me to show you how it is that one white man is to interest himself enough in this great cause to induce him to pay for the education of nine colored children along with his own." He asserted that the Delta landlord "cheerfully bears this burden," and expressed his confidence in the ability of the Negro to learn. He believed that agricultural schools should be established for the instruction of the colored race.

The legislature of 1886 passed a resolution endorsing the 'Blair Bill' then before Congress, and urging the senators and congressmen representing the state to support it. [4] This bill provided for the extension of federal aid for the education of the Negro. The *Mississippi Teacher*, August, 1889, stated that the entire delegation in Congress favored the bill, and mentioned the names of Lamar and George in this connection. This journal urged the teachers of the state to endorse it at their next meeting. The Raymond *Gazette* in 1887 opposed the bill. [5] When finally in 1890 the bill came before the Senate, Senator George voted for it, and Senator Walthall voted against it.

While these bits of evidence show decidedly that there was a strong public sentiment in favor of Negro education, there is other evidence which shows that there was developing a considerable sentiment in opposition to taxing the white people to support it. In 1889 Superintendent Preston found it necessary to satisfy a certain political element that the present limits of the school age—five to twenty-one—did not work to the advantage of the colored race. [6]

The trend of the discussion of the Article on Education, when it came up for adoption before the Constitutional Convention of 1890,

[3] Report of Superintendent, 1888–1889; 1891–1893, p. 554.
[4] House Journal, 1886, p. 233.
[5] Raymond *Gazette*, January 29, 1887.
[6] Report of Superintendent, 1888–1889, p. 11.

is perhaps the truest index of public opinion on this subject. The Committee on Education on August 28 presented a majority report on the Article.[7] Shortly afterward, a minority report signed by six members was handed in,[8] which objected in particular to a section which proposed to make an annual state distribution to the schools of $750,000. The argument in part reads as follows:

> The people are willing to maintain a free school system at a reasonable expense; but under present conditions, with a large majority of the educable children belonging to a race which differs from that which pays the cost, a race which contributes but a small part of the moneys called for, which seeks to grow yearly more and more alienated from our own, it is not to be expected that our people will fail to look with a jealous eye on the creation and distribution of a fund so enormous and so partial in its results.

This was a signal for a wrestle with substitutes and amendments which continued at intervals for a month and a half. In considering the section on the distribution of the school fund, Dr. Robinson, of Rankin, at different times offered two amendments providing for the division of the fund between the schools of the races in proportion to the amount of the taxes paid.[9] The first he withdrew to propose a substitute which, with an amendment by Mr. Dillard, was adopted as Section 206. After securing the passage of this fatal section, Robinson, still bent on a division of the funds between the races, proposed an additional section having this in view. It was defeated by a vote of eighty-one to thirty-one.[9]

There were further attempts to accomplish a division of the funds. Noland, of Wilkinson, proposed to divide county and separate district funds on this basis.[10] Magruder proposed to have special county and separate district funds so divided.[11] His amendment was defeated by a vote of fifty-seven to fifty-three, twenty-three being absent. An attempt to make the minimum limit of the school age seven instead of five, with the ostensible purpose of discriminating against the Negroes, was defeated by a vote of sixty-seven to thirty-eight.[12]

[7] Journal of Constitutional Convention, 1890, p. 118.
[8] *Ibid.*, p. 131.
[9] *Ibid.*, pp. 329, 337, 355.
[10] *Ibid.*, p. 345.
[11] *Ibid.*
[12] *Ibid.*, p. 329.

Taken as a whole, the discussion indicates that there were two well-defined factions in the convention, one which favored giving the Negro at least the educational advantages which he had heretofore enjoyed, the other which favored giving him only such as he was able to pay for with the taxes which he contributed. The first of these factions was in control, and may be called the conservative element. The second faction, however, was able to muster up a considerable following, as is evident by the votes on the Robinson and Magruder amendments.

As a further index of public opinion, we may note just here the division of the legislature on the subject of the distribution of the school fund. It would be unfair to say that those who favored distributing the school fund on a basis other than that of school population, were opposed to the education of the Negro. Superintendent Preston, Governor Stone, and Superintendent Kincannon were outspoken in favor of Negro education, but all were opposed to the adopted means of distribution. Again, we may naturally suppose that the counties which were discriminated against by this measure, would oppose it; and that those counties in whose favor it worked, would uphold it, regardless of their attitude toward Negro education. Yet, the agitation to change the means of distribution, which unquestionably increased in vehemence throughout this period, carried with it an increasing disposition to make the Negro pay for his own education. This is borne out by the statement of Superintendent Kincannon, quoted elsewhere, and by an amendment proposed in the legislature in 1896. [13]

In answer to the question of the state superintendent as to the state of public opinion (1891–1893), twelve county superintendents reported opposition to Negro education. [14] The counties represented in these reports were Carroll, Franklin, Grenada, Holmes, Jefferson, Lowndes, Lawrence, Marshall, Noxubee, Pike, Sharkey, Yalobusha. Among the reasons assigned for opposition were: "We are paying out too much money to educate the Negro," "whites complain that they have been taxed enough to support Negro schools," "want of confidence in the education of the Negro." One superintendent referred to what he called a growing disposition for each race to educate its own children; another claimed that the whites were

[13] See Distribution of the School Fund, page 95.
[14] Report of Superintendent, 1891–1893, Narrative Reports.

entitled to a longer term. It must be remembered that these reports came from only twelve out of seventy counties. Whether or not sentiment in other counties favored public education of the Negro we have no means of finding out.

The *State Ledger*, in 1892,[15] complained of the new system of apportionment which had been changed "for the advantage of the blacks, and in many instances, to the detriment of the white counties."

Despite protests, we may be sure that there was a large element that favored giving the Negro proper educational facilities. The teaching profession of this period, as of every other period which we are to consider, have left record of their confidence in Negro education. A prominent teacher, speaking before the State Teachers' Association in 1894, said in part:[16]

. . . if we want to suppress crime so prevalent among our black neighbors, and make useful and respected citizens of them, and get them to look at life from a Caucasian standpoint, we must employ more efficient teachers for them, encourage an educational spirit among them, and lengthen out their school term, so as to give them 140 days during the year for school.

A little later in the same speech the speaker touched upon the question of apportionment and expressed himself as follows:

The eyes of the South were fixed on Mississippi during the last legislature to see what disposition of the question it would make, and be it said to the eternal praise of that body, that they decided to distribute the money collected from the people equally among the two races *per capita*.

Superintendent Kincannon, in 1899, stating his position on the apportionment question, said:[17]

Do not understand, please, that I would take from any child, white or black, in the state, that which the constitution intends that he should have, for I believe that education is the panacea for nearly all the ills from which society suffers.

By way of summarizing the public sentiment of the white people for the period between 1886 and 1900, we may say: (1) that the controlling element in state politics were unwilling for any discrimination to be practised upon the Negro; (2) that the State Department of Education and the State Teachers' Association con-

[15] *State Ledger*, April 5, 1892.
[16] Proceedings, Mississippi Teachers' Association, 1894, p. 27.
[17] Report of Superintendent, 1898–1899, p. 30

sistently favored the education of the race; (3) that the need of industrial education for the Negro seems to have interested a few educators; (4) that there was hostility to Negro education between 1890 and 1900 which seems to have increased in intensity with the unrest due to an unsatisfactory means of distributing the school fund.

Public Sentiment Since 1900. We have called attention to the agitation for the division of the school fund which accompanied the demand for a more equitable distribution among the counties. This agitation seemed to increase in intensity through the nineties and the early years of the new century. The conservative element seems easily to have prevented all attempts to discriminate against Negro schools by taking away their support. Such an attempt was thwarted in the legislature in 1896, and again in 1900.[18]   But in blocking these attempts the conservatives seem to have blocked all efforts tending toward an equitable division of the school funds.

The chief exponent of the political element which favored a division of the school fund on the basis of the amount of tax paid, or at least favored devoting a large part of the school fund to the education of the white children, was Major Vardaman.   It would be well just here to have a statement of his position in his own words: [19]

Certainly, the education suited to the white children does not suit the Negro. This has been demonstrated by forty years of experience and the expenditure in the southern states of nearly $300,000,000. It was natural and quite reasonable, immediately after the Civil War, especially by those who had made but a superficial study of the Negro, to expect that freedom, equal educational facilities, and the example of the white man, would have the effect of improving his morals and make a better man of him generally. But it has not, I am sorry to say. As a race, he is deteriorating morally every day. . . The state for many years, at great expense to the tax-payers, has maintained a system of Negro education, which has produced disappointing results, and I am opposed to the perpetuation of the system. My idea is that the character of Negro education should be changed. . . There must be a moral sub-stratum upon which to build, or you cannot make a desirable citizen. The Negro is devoid of that element. . . The first step toward the changing of the education system of the state, so as to meet the demands of both races, it occurs to me, is for the legislature to

[18] See page 96.
[19] Inaugural Address, Senate Journal, 1904, p. 123.

submit to the people a proposition to amend the constitution, so as to give the legislature unrestricted authority in dealing with the public school question.

Vardaman's political opponents regarded his scheme as unjust and unconstitutional, as well as inexpedient.[20]   The press of the state seems generally to have supported the conservatives. To such an extent did the newspapers oppose Vardaman, that Noel, one of his opponents for the governorship, was charged with having subsidized the press, but the charge was not substantiated.[21]

The legislature of 1904 did not act upon the recommendation of Governor Vardaman to amend Section 206 so as to leave the distribution of the school funds in the hands of the legislature.   Nor did the next legislature accomplish anything in this direction.   In his last biennial message the Governor said:[22] "Why the Legislature should hesitate to submit to the people an amendment to the constitution so as to change the absurd and expensive system in vogue, is an inscrutable mystery to me."

Although the Governor was unable to have the method of distributing the school fund changed, he was able to use his veto power toward helping to carry out his theory in regard to Negro education. When the bill appropriating money for the support of the Holly Springs State Normal College came up for his signature, he placed his veto on it.   This bill had passed the House by a vote of seventy to nineteen, and the Senate by a vote of twenty-five to thirteen. Vardaman sent the bill back to the House with a three-page veto message, which further elaborates his view on the subject of Negro education.[23]   He said in part:

Literary education—the knowledge of books—does not seem to produce any good substantial results with the Negro, but serves to sharpen his cunning, breeds hopes that cannot be fulfilled, inspires aspirations that cannot be gratified, creates an inclination to avoid labor, promotes indolence, and in turn leads to crime. . . I wish it understood that my objection to this bill does not grow out of a spirit of race hatred. I have no such feeling for the Negro; on the contrary, I wish the race well. I should like to see it develop along moral and industrial lines, until it shall become a positive

[20] *Times-Democrat* report of Noel's Chautauqua address, July 23, 1903; also Longino's
     Inaugural Address.
[21] *Times-Democrat*, July 20, 1903, Noel's campaign notice.
[22] Biennial Message, Senate Journal, 1908, p. 10.
[23] House Journal, 1904, p. 840.

factor for good, rather than a menace to civilization; a blessing rather than a curse.

The veto message was made the special order for March 15. An attempt in the House to pass the appropriation bill over the governor's veto resulted in a vote of sixty-four to forty-eight, twenty-one absent, and thus failed to secure the necessary majority of two-thirds.

A committee of five appointed by the State Teachers' Association in 1901, rendered an elaborate report to the Association on May 1, 1903. In discussing the factors which tended to deter the growth of rural education they expressed themselves as follows:[24]

Probably no other one thing acts as such a drawback to general progress, and especially to educational progress in Mississippi, as does this presence of an inferior race, not willing or able to bear any considerable portion of the burden of taxation; but which, owing to its large numbers, under the operation of existing laws receives so large a part of the public funds for education. The dominant race is not willing to vote money to be expended for the schools of the inferior race. It is not in the province of the Committee to say whether or not this indisposition to educate the Negro is proper. Certain it is that Doctor Alderman's statement, "The Negro must be educated, ignorance is no remedy for anything; any other theory is monstrous," ought to receive the most careful consideration at the hands of all those who have the shaping of the educational policy of the state.

Continuing its report of the situation the committee said that the indisposition of the whites to tax themselves for the benefit of the Negro had led to apathy in regard to education; that local taxation had almost disappeared except in the separate districts; and that the state fund was furnishing the entire support of rural schools.

The question of the education of the Negro came before the State Teachers' Association again in 1905, when the president devoted a section of his address to a discussion of the subject. His position may be summarized in his own words:[25]

Whenever the question of raising additional revenue for educational purposes is discussed, we are met with opposition on account of: First, the failure of our present schools to improve the condition of the Negro—this I am compelled to admit is largely true; not the fault of education *per se*, but rather a failure of our methods for the Negro; second, the opinion of most people that the Negro is now receiving the larger proportion of our school

[24] Report of Superintendent, 1901–1903, p. 69.
[25] Proceedings, State Teachers' Association, 1905, President's Address

appropriation, when in fact, the opposite is true. . . The discussion of the education of the Negro has always been carefully avoided in this association, being considered as a political, rather than an educational question; but I believe the advancement of the educational interests of our state depends, in great measure, upon the proper solution of this question; therefore, as an association we should give some consideration to this important part of our educational system.

In concluding his remarks on this subject the president said that the Negro should have schools specially adapted to his needs. He characterized the attempt to give him a classical education as "giving a stone to him who asks for bread." He advocated an entirely different course of study for Negro schools, a course limited on the intellectual side to the 'three R's', but strong on the industrial and moral sides. No action seems to have been taken by the Association on this subject.

Among the most esteemed citizens of the state within recent years was Bishop Charles B. Galloway, the great orator-churchman-statesman. Bishop Galloway served for a number of years on the board of trustees of Alcorn College, and showed his interest in the education of the Negro in a number of ways. He may be regarded as the spokesman of a large number of people when he says:[26]

. . . I believe the dominant desire of our people has been to deal justly and do right. And wherein we have failed the fault has not been all our own. . . . And any policy which tends to inflame prejudice and widen the racial chasm postpones indefinitely the final triumph of the Son of Man among the sons of men. . . I do insist that the Negro have equal opportunity with every American citizen.

We may conclude from these bits of evidence: (1) that there was a tendency on the part of a large number of people to resent taxation for the support of Negro schools; (2) that the controlling element in state politics seems not to have been inclined toward radical action; (3) that lack of confidence in the results of the work of the public schools for Negroes seems to have developed in the minds of many; (4) that an increasing tendency to favor moral and industrial education for the Negro is evident; (5) that a large number of the population favored giving the Negro an opportunity for education and dealing justly with him in every particular.

[26] Jackson *Evening News*, June 3, 1903; Speech at the laying of corner-stone of the new Capitol.

CHAPTER XI

THE INFLUENCE OF EDUCATION UPON THE LIFE OF THE NEGRO

It has been frequently asserted that education has had little or no influence upon the social and economic progress of the Negro race. Indeed, some observers have gone so far as to say that the education the Negro has received has been positively detrimental. Much that has been said upon this subject is mere assertion and has not been subjected to scientific verification. A careful scientific study is needed to clarify the matter, but, on account of the scarcity of data, it is doubtful if a very complete study is possible. In this chapter I have attempted in a fragmentary manner to explain the social and economic progress—or lack of progress—of the race, in the light of the educational history of the state.

By way of introduction, it would be well to point out the difficulty which awaits one who attempts to place educational opportunities and social progress in the relation of cause and effect. For instance, to say that a marked social advance in one generation came in response to a liberal provision for education in the generation next preceding, may be true, but there is a chance that other factors contributed largely to bring about the advance. Conversely, to say that lack of progress is due to a lack of educational facilities, or to a false conception of education, is to state what may prove to be but a half-truth. Yet, if, as in the present instance, we analyze a total situation, and find in several selected lines of social activity a close parallelism with educational conditions, we are probably justified in placing the two in the relation of cause and effect.

Then also we must be on our guard lest we expect too much of education extending over only a short period. Social progress, particularly in the case of a backward race, moves by slow degrees and may better be measured in centuries than in years. But to deny the power of education to function perceptibly in one generation is almost to deny the power of the human mind to respond to training.

Has education improved the living conditions of the Negro race? In what ways have the educational facilities provided by the state of Mississippi brought about race progress? Among the things that make for social betterment and race progress we may mention ownership of homes; acquisition of farm property including lands, domestic animals, and implements; increase in the number of farm managers; increase in the membership of the professional classes; decrease in crime. Reliable statistical information is available for an investigation along these lines. Possibly the investigation might be extended along other lines but I have not found available data. My study will therefore be restricted to the aforementioned topics.

Ownership of Homes. Ownership of homes is one of the truest indications of economic efficiency. Besides, it is one of the most important factors in the health problem.[1] Hence, if education functions at all it should function in economic efficiency leading to home ownership. Has this been the case? Something near the correct answer to this question might be obtained by a comparison of home ownership and facilities for education at intervals of ten years for the entire period of our study. But I have not found statistics available for such a comparison. The few statistics which I have found indicate a very high correlation between generally meager school facilities and small accumulation of home property.

During the decade between 1900 and 1910 there was a slight increase in the ownership of homes by Negroes, as well as an increase in the number free from encumbrance.[2] In 1900, there was one owned home to every 31.3 persons, or a total of 28,855; in 1910, there was one owned home to every 26.3 persons, or a total of 38,564. Or, taking a different view of the matter, in 1900 the owned homes represented 15 per cent. of all homes, and in 1910 they represented 16.9 per cent. This increase of 1.9 per cent. for Mississippi was somewhat less than the average for the south Atlantic states and for the east south central states. From whatever view taken, the ownership of homes by Negroes is relatively small and has not progressed as rapidly as might be desired.

With respect to encumbrance, there were somewhat fewer homes under mortgage in 1910 than in 1900. Of the owned homes, 59 per cent. were free of encumbrance in 1900, and 60.5 per cent. in 1910.

[1] A Special Report of the United States Census in 1916, entitled *Negroes in the United States* (p. 46), says: "Undoubtedly one of the factors which have caused the decrease in the death rate—which decrease is almost universal in the cities of the South—is the increase in home ownership among the Negro population."

[2] *Negroes in the United States*, pp. 29, 104.

The statistics we have so far cited include both 'farm homes' and 'other homes'. The Negroes have been far more fortunate in the acquisition of homes as domiciles than as farms. While the number of farm homes increased from 20,939 to 24,791, or 18.6 per cent., the other homes increased from 7,916 to 13,783, or 74.1 per cent. The relatively heavy expense of purchasing land enough to provide a living has evidently prohibited many Negroes from this form of ownership.

Facts probably more significant from the standpoint of education, are statistics of home ownership in cities of a population of 5,000 and over. The best schools in the state have undoubtedly been the city schools supervised by the city superintendents. As throwing light upon the educational situation for the state as a whole, the consideration of the influence of city schools is of slight consequence, since there are only five towns in the state with a Negro population exceeding 5,000, and the total Negro population for all five is but 44,638.[3] But, as an index to the value of education with respect to home ownership, the figures are indeed suggestive. For the state at large, we find in 1910 one owned home to every 26.3 persons; in the cities, we find one to every 16.2 persons. Likewise, we find in the state as a whole 60.5 per cent. of the owned homes free of mortgage, and in the cities 73.6 per cent. If we knew to what extent the cities tend to select the best Negro element, we would have a more reliable measure of the influence of education. Certainly, it is true that the most capable Negroes tend to flock to the cities, but it is also true that many of the less capable congregate in them, induced by work in oil mills and in other manufacturing plants. If, in the absence of other data, we dare strike a balance, and say that on the average city Negroes are no better equipped by original nature than are country Negroes, the influence of the city environment and of superior school facilities is at once apparent.

In general, we may say that the backwardness of the Negro schools of the state seems to be reflected in the meager accumulation of home property. That education has been an influential factor in fitting Negroes to acquire homes is apparent when we compare home ownership in cities where good school facilities are provided with the ownership in country districts where the provision for education has been inadequate.

[3] *Negroes in the United States*, p. 106.

Progress in Agriculture. The influence of education upon the economic efficiency of the Negro can perhaps best be estimated by considering the progress he has made in the dominant industry— agriculture. Students of the Negro problem have frequently pointed with pride to the large amount of farm property which the Negro has accumulated in the short period since his emancipation. Considered in the aggregate the figures which represent this accumulation appear large, but may we not with justice raise the question whether, in proportion to the population, they are as large as they should be. We have seen that there has been little progress in the development of schools for the colored race. Are there any evidences of arrested development in agriculture probably traceable to lack of proper training and instruction? The purpose of this section of our study will be to determine the possible influence of education upon the agricultural progress of the Negro in Mississippi.

It is well for us first to consider the importance of the industry of agriculture in this state. The rural Negro population in 1890 represented 95.4 per cent. of the total Negro population. By 1910, this percentage had dropped to 90.6, but in this year, despite the percentage decrease, it showed an aggregate increase from something over 700,000 to something over 900,000. We may safely say that practically all the rural Negro population was dependent upon agriculture for a livelihood.

Significant to be observed in a study of agricultural progress with relation to education are: (1) the acquisition of farm lands; (2) the increase in the number of Negro farm managers; (3) the acquisition of farm implements and machinery; (4) the acquisition of domestic animals. We shall investigate each of these topics in the order named.

1. The Twelfth Census [4] indicates that Negroes resident in northern states have acquired property since 1860 more rapidly than their southern brothers. In the south Atlantic states Negroes have acquired property about three-fourths as rapidly as the whites in that section; and in the south central states only about half as rapidly as the whites. Mississippi, as representative of the south central states, has doubtless furnished fewer opportunities for the acquisition of farm property than have many of her neighboring states.

[4] Twelfth Census, Vol. V, p. cvii.

Despite the fact that more farms are operated by Negroes in Mississippi than in any other state, and despite the fact that there are more Negro farm owners than in any other state except Virginia, the Negroes, in proportion to the population, have made relatively slow progress in acquiring farms.[5] This is true in particular of the last decade of our study. In 1900, 61.1 per cent. of the white farmers owned their farms, and in 1910, 66.3 per cent. In 1900, only 15.2 per cent. of the colored farmers owned their farms, and in 1910, only 16.3 per cent. It is evident from these figures that the relative increase in farm ownership for the colored race has been very small.

The Twelfth Census also gives a special statistical study which proves that Negroes in the black belts accumulate property very slowly.[6] This study is particularly significant for Mississippi since by far the greater part of the Negro population is concentrated in the black belt. From each of seven states,[7] black belts of fifteen counties were selected for comparison with a similarly selected group of white counties in each state. The farms operated by Negroes in each group of counties were classified according as they were operated by owners, by managers, and by tenants. In the resulting statistical display, Mississippi stood third among the states in percentage of Negro farm owners. But when the fifteen counties representing the black belts were considered separately, the state stood seventh in the list, only eight per cent. of the farms being operated by owners. The black belt of Mississippi is thus shown to be the least favorable place in seven states for the accumulation of farm property by Negroes. In the white counties of the state conditions were far more favorable. Here 38.4 per cent. of the farms were owned by the individuals who operated them.

[5] The *Negro Year Book*, 1917 (pp. 305, 314), gives figures which apparently contradict this statement. It shows that the increase in the number of farms operated by Negroes in Mississippi during the decade between 1900 and 1910 was thirty-eight per cent., that the average increase for the South was twenty per cent., and that only four states exceeded this record of Mississippi. It showed further that the aggregate number of Negro farm owners in the state exceeded that of all other states except Virginia. These figures, given in the aggregate, hardly represent the true situation. Instead of attempting to compare Mississippi with other states with respect to the aggregate increase, I have used as the basis for computing progress the ratio of farm owners to farm operatives of each race.

[6] Twelfth Census, Vol. V, p. cix.

[7] The seven states were: Alabama, Arkansas, Georgia, Louisiana, Mississippi, South Carolina, and Texas.

I do not intend to argue upon this basis that more favorable educational conditions in the white counties made the Negroes therein more thrifty. We have elsewhere shown that school facilities were possibly no better in white counties than in black counties. The high percentage of Negro owners in the white counties may be accounted for by the fact that lands there are cheaper; and by the fact that Delta land-owners dispose of land only in large tracts. Perhaps also the law of the survival of the fittest has operated. Since poor lands make it difficult to secure a living in the white counties, the less thrifty have migrated to the rich Delta plantations where the tenant system furnishes large returns for little labor. This theory is supported by statistics which indicate that the black counties are becoming blacker, and that the white counties are becoming whiter.[8] These statistics, therefore, can hardly be interpreted as a reflection of educational conditions, except in so far as we may note the parallel in generally poor school facilities and generally meager ownership of farm property in the section of the state containing about eighty per cent. of the Negro population.

2. It might be expected that statistics indicating the progress of the Negro as a manager of farms would reflect economic efficiency attained by schooling. The practice, however, of employing managers for farms has not been very general in Mississippi, and is evidently on the decline. Even when managers are employed, white men are secured in about seven cases out of eight. White managers, in 1900, numbered 823 to 107 colored; in 1910, they numbered only 719 to 106 colored. The Negro apparently has gained only a foothold in this occupation, and is barely able to hold his own in it.

The objection to Negro managers lies chiefly in the fact that they have rarely developed power to control the laborers of their own color. The fault lies partly in the lack of executive ability of the managers, and partly in the suspicion of their ignorant laboring brothers. Further training might gain for the Negro a place in this occupation, but such as he has had has not resulted in making him a factor of great consequence as a farm manager in Mississippi.

3. Very little of service in this connection can be learned from the available statistics of ownership of domestic animals.[9] Domestic animals, especially horses, mules, and cattle, are frequently rented

[8] United States Commissioner's Report, 1901, Vol. I, p. 740.
[9] Twelfth Census; Abstract of the Thirteenth Census, Mississippi Supplement.

by farm tenants or cared for by them with the consent of the owner or landlord. The census reports do not indicate the number of animals owned by tenants, but simply the number on farms under the care of the tenants. Hence it is difficult to estimate progress in this form of ownership. The statistics which we have, indicate a notable increase in the number of cattle (probably) owned by Negroes. They indicate also that during the decade between 1900 and 1910 Negroes apparently outstripped the whites in progress in hog-raising, but that neither race progressed very much.

A reliable test of economic efficiency is the ability of a farmer to diversify his products. Farmers in Mississippi have not been much inclined to diversify. They have preferred rather to raise a single crop, sell it, and, from the proceeds, to purchase the things they need for home consumption. Recently, however, there has been an agitation to induce them to make their farms self-sufficient by planting forage crops and raising hogs, cattle, and other animals. It would be interesting to present facts showing the extent to which Negroes have responded to the call for diversification. Unfortunately there are no available figures on the subject. We know that there are fewer swine on the average Negro farm than on the average white farm, and that Negroes have never taken to the raising of sheep, goats, and bees. Aside from these bits of information we know very little.

From what we are able to gather, the education the Negro has received has not resulted in an appreciable increase in the ownership of domestic animals.

The introduction of improved farm implements and machinery is a true index, under ordinary circumstances, of the economic efficiency of farmers. The increased value of farm implements ought to be a fairly accurate measure of progress. According to the census reports (1900 and 1910) the Negro farmers have kept pace with white farmers in the acquisition of farm implements. Here again we have to discount the figures. Many Negro tenants work on shares and contract with their employers to furnish the tools to be used. Doubtless many of the implements reported from Negro farms belong to white landlords. Education may have induced a number of farmers of the Negro race to invest in improved machinery, but to what extent this is true we have no means of ascertaining.

In concluding this section on progress in agriculture we may say that, as a rule, the Negro farmers have not advanced very rapidly. It is asserted that education has not improved and will not improve them. A fair trial has never been made. A meager provision for education, and that of a kind not designed to function in economic efficiency, has produced the lazy, unprogressive farmers of the present. Enough progress has been made, however, to indicate that the education Negroes have received has not been altogether wasted. What can be done with adequate facilities and improved methods, remains to be seen.

Professional Service. Statistics indicating the increase in the number of Negroes engaged in professional service ought to prove a reliable indication of race progress. The transfer to the professions from agriculture, trade, and domestic service is directly dependent upon mental capacity, ideals, and school training. Membership in the professional classes should, therefore, reflect to a certain extent the educational facilities of the state.

A special report of the United States Census Office,[10] in 1904, gives the following figures for Mississippi. Number of Negroes engaged in the various branches of professional service in Mississippi:

Clergymen	994	Government Officials	39
Dentists	5	Physicians	45
Engineers	3	Teachers	661[11]
Journalists	6	Total in Professional Service	1,888
Lawyers	24		

It is quite evident that professional service has not enlisted a very appreciable number of Negroes in its ranks. It would be interesting to compare the figures here given with the figures for the two decades next preceding, but unfortunately I am able to furnish comparative statistics in only one or two instances. Between 1890 and 1900, the number of clergymen increased from 989 to 994; the number of lawyers decreased from 26 to 24; and the number of physicians increased from 34 to 45. In this decade, at least, professional service seems to have been practically at a standstill. The small increase in the number engaged in the teaching profession (see Statistical Summary, p. 141) during the same period is significant in this connection.

[10] United States Census, Occupations, 1904.
[11] This number probably represents the number of males engaged in teaching.

Of course, it cannot be positively asserted that, since few Negroes are engaged in professional service in Mississippi, the preliminary training provided in the schools has been deficient. Doubtless many native Negroes have entered the professions and migrated elsewhere. Doubtless also, the emigration of the educated classes has exceeded the immigration. The social level of the race, however, is largely determined by the number engaged in professional service, since the lower orders of society generally look to the professions for leadership. We may say, finally, that, to the extent school training can modify the life callings of individuals, the education the Mississippi Negro has received has apparently not directed him into professional service.

The Negro and Crime. It was the contention of the early organizers of the Mississippi school system that education would reduce criminality. Many Southerners who at first were reluctant to shoulder the expensive responsibility of Negro schools were somewhat reconciled to their burden by the prospect of a safer and more orderly society. Whenever Negro education has been advocated the argument that it would make the race more law-abiding has been brought forward.

In more recent times Senator Vardaman and other observers of Negro life have expressed the opinion that the education the Negro has received has not tended to lift him to a higher level of morality. In the face of this contention we may well raise the question whether or not forty years of education—or lack of proper education—have tended to improve the status of the Negro in the eyes of the law. In our attempt to answer this question we shall let the statistics in the reports of the superintendent of the state penitentiary speak for themselves. These figures do not furnish all the information we desire, but such as is given provides the basis for some very definite conclusions.

In answer to the question whether or not literacy tends to diminish crime we offer the following data: Of the reports examined, only the one for 1909–1911 tabulates the number of illiterate criminals. In this year, we find that 944 of the 1,834 inmates of the penitentiary were illiterate, and that 28 others were unable to write. Of the total population ten years of age and over in Mississippi, 22.4 per cent. are illiterate. We find, therefore, that over 50 per cent. of the criminals are coming from an illiterate population representing but 22.4 per cent. of the whole. It seems clear that literacy and keeping out of jail go together. To what extent this generalization will apply to the Negro we can but draw our own inference, since literate and illiterate criminals are not classified according to race in the report.

I have collected and tabulated the most significant facts in the reports of the superintendent of the state penitentiary. These facts are presented in Table VIII. In the study of this table we are hampered by the fact that the crimes committed by the criminals of each race are not specified. But since such a large proportion of the criminals belong to the Negro race, we are reasonably safe in drawing inferences with respect to the race from the figures as given. A point that will probably occur to the reader as striking is the slump in the prison population in 1890. The superintendent accounts for this by calling attention to the raising of the limit of the fine for petty larceny from ten to twenty-five dollars.[12] The conclusions which we will draw, however, need not be affected by the exceptionally low figures for this year.

A number of facts brought out in Table VIII strike us with startling effect:

1. Although the Negro population of Mississippi has, during the three decades of the study, represented but fifty-six per cent. of the total population, it has furnished nine-tenths of the criminals.

2. The number of Negro convicts has increased 84.6 per cent. in thirty years, paralleling an increase in the total Negro population of 55.2. The number of white convicts has increased 77.1 per cent., paralleling an increase in the white population of 64 per cent.

3. Crimes against property in 1880 were twice as numerous as crimes against the person; in 1910, the opposite was true, the crimes against property representing scarcely fifty per cent. of the crimes against the person.

4. With respect to the particular crimes for which the criminals were sentenced, we note that for every case of murder and for every case of manslaughter recorded in 1880, there were *five* recorded in 1910. The increase in the population may modify these figures, but it can by no means rob them of their terrible truth.

5. There were almost three times the number of cases of rape in 1910 than there were thirty years before. The number of cases

[12] Report of Superintendent of Penitentiary, 1890, p. 13.

practically doubled between 1900 and 1910. The number of cases of attempted rape also was multiplied threefold in thirty years.[13]

6. There were three cases of assault in 1910 to one in 1880.

7. Larceny is apparently on the decline, and robbery and burglary on the increase.

TABLE VIII

CRIMINALS IN THE MISSISSIPPI PENITENTIARY

(*Statistics Compiled from Reports of the Superintendent*)

	1910[14]	*1900*[15]	*1890*[16]	*1880*[17]
Total number of convicts	1,834	910	485	997
Number of colored convicts	1,671	823	435	905
Number of white convicts	163	87	50	92
TOTAL CRIMES AGAINST PROPERTY[18]	518	311	177	622
Grand larceny	139	98	75	323
Larceny	29			111
Forgery	3	16	24	18
Robbery	46	26	13	12
Burglary	243	116	45	92
Burglary and larceny	58	55	30	66
CASES OF PERSONAL VIOLENCE[18]	1,201	517	250	270
Murder	509	175	90	95
Manslaughter	374	166	75	70
Assault to kill, rob, or rape	221	110	54	72
Attempted rape	56	45	14	17
Rape	41	21	17	16
CRIMES UNDER OTHER TITLES	115	82	58	105

[13] Doubtless a large number of the cases of rape represented by these commitments were crimes against Negro women. See Stone: *Studies in the American Race Problem*, p. 97.

[14] Based on number of convicts, July 1, 1911.

[15] Based on number of convicts, September 30, 1900.

[16] Based on number of convicts, December 4, 1890.

[17] Figures based on number of convicts, December 1, 1879.

[18] Represents total of crimes in this grouping committed by convicts in State Penitentiary.

8. Forgery, an offense dependent upon a certain amount of school training, has never carried many Negroes in this state to the penitentiary, and now shows a slight tendency toward declining.

In furnishing an unduly large proportion of criminals from the Negro race, Mississippi is not an exception among the states of the Union. Nor is the alarming increase in crime among Negroes exceptional in the case of Mississippi. Professor Walter F. Wilcox in 1899 pointed out the fact [19] that Negro criminality was increasing faster in northern than in southern states. The *Negro Year Book* [20] for 1917 indicates that the same tendencies have continued down to the present.

More notable, perhaps, than anything else is the rapid increase in the number of crimes involving personal violence. It would be interesting to know to what extent the commitments have been made for difficulties involving race antagonism, but the statistics throw no light on this phase of the subject. The truth is that Negroes are acquiring more respect for property and are tending to respect persons less. Is this not a problem for education, at least for an educational experiment?

The apparent increase in crime in Mississippi may perhaps be extenuated by the fact that the courts have become increasingly more vigilant. Probably also, Negroes have tended more and more to bring their grievances into court. On the other hand, it is fair to surmise that murders and manslaughters have at all times found their way into the courts, and that the increase indicated by the figures comes very near representing the truth for these crimes.

Professor Wilcox claims that the primary cause of crime is defective family life and training.[21] Hence, he declares, crime is most common during the years just after the child has passed out from the control of the family, while he is finding himself ill-adapted by training for the new sphere of life. Statistics for Mississippi bear him out in his conclusion. In 1890, 272, or nearly half of the 485 inmates of the penitentiary, were under twenty-five years of age, and 109, or nearly one-fourth, were under twenty. The same proportion holds for 1900.

[19] Stone: *Studies in the American Race Problem*, p. 443.
[20] *Negro Year Book*, 1917, p. 335.
[21] Stone: *loc. cit.*

Since defective family life seems to play an important part as a cause of crime, it would be well at this point to investigate the status of the Negro family in Mississippi.

The United States Commissioner of Labor in 1889 asserted that almost seventy-five per cent. of the divorces in the South were granted to Negroes.[22] In this statement he may have been in error because it is not always easy to estimate the number of divorces in securing census returns. Many divorced people report themselves as single, and thus tend to reduce the total. From a Special Report of the United States Census Office [23] in 1909 we learn that 41.8 per cent. of the white population of Mississippi fifteen years of age and over are married, and that 58.2 per cent. of the colored population of the same age are married. We learn also that 16.3 per cent. of all divorces were granted to whites, and 83.7 per cent. to Negroes. The percentage of divorce for the Negro race in Mississippi exceeds that of all other states. For the reason stated above, the estimate for Mississippi is probably not too high. Other statistics in the special report indicate that divorce is more prevalent in black than in white counties, and that the number of divorces is increasing.

It seems, therefore, that there is a very close correlation of defective family life and crime in Mississippi, and that the remedy will lie in the improvement of the marital relations of the Negro and in the providing of some form of education that will make up for the deficiencies of home training. Upon this subject, Professor Wilcox says [24] that the most effective safeguard against crime is the inculcation in children by their parents of the desire to work and earn a living. He adds: "If the Negro family on the average is far less effective than the white, the education provided for the Negro children should aim frankly to supplement the shortcomings of their family life and reduce their temptations to crime by increasing their desire and ability to live by legitimate industry."

Clarence H. Poe, a southern white man, in 1904 took the statistics which seemed to indicate that the Negro was becoming more criminal as he received more education, and clearly proved that the

[22] *Marriage and Divorce*, Part I, p. 21.
[23] *Ibid.*, p. 20.
[24] Stone: *Studies in the American Race Problem*, p. 448.

figures had been misinterpreted.[25]   In concluding his argument in favor of increased educational facilities for Negroes, he says:

It is plain, therefore, that even with the pitifully foolish and inefficient methods which have obtained heretofore, the schooling the Negro has had, has been helpful and not harmful.   But we must adopt a wiser policy.   Industrial education, as exemplified in Hampton and Tuskegee Institutes, strikes directly at the evils which foster crime; and to breathe the spirit of these institutions into the general public school system of the race is the imperative and immediate duty of those who have the matter in charge.   To delay in this means danger.   It is the impotence and ineptness of the old systems that have brought people to doubt the wisdom of all Negro education.   A direct result is the triumph of Governor Vardaman of Mississippi on the platform, "No white taxes to teach Negro schools."

Gilbert T. Stephenson, one of the foremost authorities on the legal status of the Negro, in 1917, adduces evidence which tends to show that the cause of crime among Negroes is lack of sufficient education of the proper kind.[26]   The small amount of education which they have received has been scarcely enough to function. Citing an estimate from the Mississippi Penitentiary, he shows that in one camp consisting of 450 Negroes about half could neither read nor write, and that less than ten per cent. of the other half had anything like a fair education.

We may say finally that the contention that crime among Negroes is increasing in Mississippi is supported by undeniable facts.   When the question is raised whether this is because of, or in spite of, the education they have received, I believe there can be but one answer. We have pointed out that twenty-two per cent. of the adult population of the state is furnishing over fifty per cent. of the criminals; we have also pointed out that Negro family life is defective, and consequently home training is deficient in a very large number of cases; we have pointed out that the school facilities which have been provided for Negro children have been far from adequate. These are causes sufficient to account for the situation.   The beneficent results of proper education as shown in the graduates of Hampton and Tuskegee may put at rest the fears of any who doubt the moral value of education.   We may admit that crime is due to deficient education, but we cannot say that literacy is the cause of

---

[25] *Atlantic Monthly*, 1904, p. 162.
[26] *South Atlantic Quarterly*, January, 1917, p. 16.

crime. Although we may well question whether formal instruction in letters and computing—the sum total of the average Negro's education—is sufficient to insure economic efficiency and sound moral life, we must refuse to believe that this instruction has been positively detrimental. Can we hope for education to function in social efficiency unless we provide definite training in morals and in the things that make for economic independence?

Summary. In concluding this chapter we do not wish to overlook the fact that in isolated cases the Negro race in Mississippi has made marked progress. Banks, newspapers, insurance companies, and other business enterprises have been organized and successfully operated by Negroes. Mound Bayou, a Negro town of about 600 inhabitants, is owned and governed exclusively by Negroes. For the masses, however, the lack of progress indicated by the statistical studies of this chapter, is typical. This lack of progress is not an argument that education has been useless, but a plea that a more ample provision be made and that the form of education be adapted to the needs of the race. In view of the meager equipment of the public schools, the short terms, the formal course of study, the ill-trained and poorly paid teachers, it would be marvelous, indeed, if greater results were forthcoming. It is trite to say that the virtual stagnation of fifty-six per cent. of the population of Mississippi constitutes a menace to the social and economic health of the state. Better facilities and specific training leading to moral and economic efficiency will alone improve the situation.

CHAPTER XII

SOCIAL AND ECONOMIC PROGRESS

Density and Distribution of the Population, and its Influence on Education. A few facts in regard to the density and distribution of the population in Mississippi will serve to throw light on the educational situation. The author has compiled a few such facts from the Twelfth and Thirteenth Censuses and placed them in tabular form in Table IX. It will be observed that the total population of the state increased in twenty years over 500,000, representing a percentage increase of about 40 per cent. During the same period the number of towns with over 2,500 inhabitants, doubled in number, and the urban population increased threefold. The density of the state increased from 27.4 persons to the square mile in 1890, to 38.2 persons to the square mile in 1910. It should be observed, however, that, in spite of the fact that there was a large increase in the urban population, and in spite of the fact that the rural population was relatively less in 1910 than in 1890, there was an absolute increase of over 300,000 in the number of country people.

Both white and colored races seem to have shared the increase almost equally, although the white population increased somewhat more rapidly than the colored race during the last decade. It is evident that the Negro population in Mississippi is still the dominant racial element in respect to numbers. Mississippi and South Carolina are the only two southern states where this is true. In 1900, among the states of the Union, Mississippi had the second largest Negro population. In thirty-eight of the seventy-nine counties, the Thirteenth Census shows that half the inhabitants were Negroes; in seventeen counties three-fourths of the inhabitants were Negroes; in Issaquena County 94.2 per cent. of the population were of the colored race.

These facts bring home to us the truth that the educational problem in Mississippi is largely a rural problem. They suggest the difficulties which confront the state in its efforts to provide educational facilities for a population so widely distributed. They sug-

gest, further, the burden which must be imposed upon the white tax-
payers, if they are to provide equal educational facilities not only
for their own children, but also for the children of the colored race.

TABLE IX

DENSITY AND DISTRIBUTION OF POPULATION, 1890–1910

(Compiled from United States Census Reports)

	1910	*1900*	*1890*
Total population	1,797,114	1,551,270	1,289,600
Number of towns over 2,500	24	22	12
Population of towns over 2,500	207,311	120,035	69,966
Population of country	1,589,803	1,431,235	1,219,634
Per cent. city	11.5	7.7	5.4
Per cent. rural	88.5	92.3	94.6
Number of people per square mile	38.2	33.1	27.4
Total white population	786,111	641,200	544,851
Total colored population	1,009,487	907,630	742,559
Per cent. white	43.7	41.3	42.4
Per cent. colored	56.2	58.5	57.6

Illiteracy. The illiteracy situation in Mississippi is summarized
in the Thirteenth Census:[1]

There are 290,235 illiterates in the state, representing 22.4 per cent. of
the total population ten years of age and over, as compared with 32 per cent.
in 1900. The percentage of illiteracy is 35.6 among the Negroes, 15.1 among
foreign-born whites, and 5.2 among native whites. It is 5.3 for native whites
of native parentage and 2.2 for native whites of foreign and mixed parentage.

For each class of the population the percentage of illiterates in the rural
population greatly exceeds that in the urban; and for all classes combined
the percentage is 23.8 in the rural population as against 13 in the urban. For
persons from ten to twenty years, inclusive, whose illiteracy depends largely
upon present school facilities and school attendance, the percentage of illiteracy is 14.4.

Here again we meet a rural problem and a problem of educating
the colored population. The illiteracy among native whites is rela-

[1] Thirteenth Census, 1910, Population, p. 1038.

tively small, and that among foreign-born whites does not constitute a menace, since Mississippi receives a very small number of immigrants from foreign countries.

With particular reference to the Negro race we observe that 25.7 per cent. of the urban population and 36.8 per cent. of the rural population are illiterate. It seems clear that the fault lies mainly in lack of facilities for instruction in rural communities.[2]

That the school system is still not more than two-thirds as efficient as it should be, is indicated by the fact that in 1910 only 63.7 per cent. of the Negro children between the ages of six and fourteen were in school. However, we must concede the fact that much has been done with meager facilities toward equipping Negroes with a knowledge of reading and writing.

Economic Development. From the figures in the accompanying table it is evident that there was a very small increase in the wealth of the state from 1886 to 1899. In fact, the assessed valuation of property in 1899 was still below the assessed valuation in 1870 when the school system was established.[3] By comparing the figures here given with those given at the beginning of this study (page 3) we find that the state as late as 1909 was only three-fifths as wealthy as it was before the Civil War.

	1909	*1899*	*1886*
Value of realty	$231,889,588	$113,210,931	$88,496,483
Value of personal property	109,928,544	48,258,651	40,702,561
Value of real and personal property	341,818,132	161,469,582	129,199,044

The greater part of the wealth of the state has consisted of farm property. The census of 1910 tells the story of the increase in this form of wealth in the following words:[4] "The total value of farm property increased during the last ten years by $222,094,000, or 108.8 per cent. To this total increase, $182,155,000 was contributed to by land and buildings; $32,590,000 by live stock; and

[2] *Negroes in the United States*, pp. 100–102.
[3] The author is aware that assessed value is not always true value, but in the present instance it is the only available means of estimating value.
[4] Abstract of Census, 1910, Mississippi Supplement, p. 612.

$7,349,000 by implements and machinery. The total absolute gain was more than six times as great, and the total percentage gain nearly five times as great between 1900 and 1910, as during the decade immediately preceding." We may add by way of explanation that between 1880 and 1890 the value of farm property increased only 37.1 per cent.; and between 1890 and 1900, only 22 per cent.

It is clear that the state has been slow to recover from the economic demoralization which succeeded the Civil War. During the first three decades of our study very little progress was made. With the opening of the new century, however, progress has been made by leaps and bounds.

Evidences of the struggle the state was having in its efforts to meet the ever-increasing demands of the schools, are not wanting. Complaints against heavy taxation were being continuously raised. In 1882, the school fund was increased $100,000 by legislative enactment, and the state tax was decreased from three to two and one-half mills. This caused a deficit, [5] and brought about retrenchment in 1888. In 1897, the six-mill tax levy failed to meet the legislative appropriations, and the schools stood in danger of being closed. [6] The governor had to call a special session of the legislature to remedy the situation. Crop failures and epidemics of yellow fever from year to year contributed to the demoralization.

The state school fund in 1886, including fines and forfeitures, retained in the counties, amounted to $335,551.23; by 1899, it had increased to $675,645.78; and by 1909, to $1,249,516.64. The schools were therefore demanding in 1909 four times as much as in 1886. These figures seem to indicate that the demands of the schools were increasing more rapidly than the ability to pay.

As increased economic prosperity resulted in the improvement of school facilities, so, in turn, increased efficiency in the school system has doubtless tended to augment economic prosperity. Within the last ten years conditions of rural life have improved wonderfully. Good roads, rural free delivery, telephones, diversified farming have contributed to the forward movement. Mississippi is now demonstrating her faith in public education by appropriating, year by year, larger and larger sums for its support.

[5] Message of Governor Lowry, January 5, 1888.
[6] House Journal, Extra Session, 1897, Message of Governor, p. 8.

CHAPTER XIII

CONCLUSIONS

I. *In an agricultural state, so sparsely settled as Mississippi, the burden of maintaining separate schools for the two races has been extremely heavy.*

1. The burden has been all the more heavy because the state has been slow to recover from the demoralization of the Civil War, and to establish itself upon a new economic basis.

2. The burden became increasingly heavy with the awakening of the white people to the benefits to be derived from public education. This was certainly true down to 1900.

3. With the increase of the educational wants of the white race, the white people have become more and more jealous of the amount that was required to defray the cost of Negro schools.

4. The inequitable method of distributing the school fund among the counties has caused the tax-payers of certain counties to feel that they were being discriminated against, and to believe that the Negro schools—more specifically the black counties—were drawing more than their proportionate share of the state's revenues.

5. Although loud complaints have been raised against the taxation of the whites to support Negro schools, a conservative element has in most instances controlled the legislative assemblies and prevented action which might have proved disastrous to Negro schools.

II. *Public sentiment in regard to the education of the Negro has been divided. One wing has regarded education as a social necessity; another has held that the cost of the education of the colored race was greater than the returns that came from it.*

1. During the first decade after the close of the Civil War, southern leaders seem generally to have favored the education of the Negro. The opposition to public education which developed during this period seems to have been directed more against the abuses of its administration under the Reconstructionists than against the education of the Negro. Among the southern leaders who were outspoken in their belief in the education of the Negro, were Governor Hum-

phreys, Senator J. Z. George, Governor Stone, and State Superintendents Joseph Bardwell and Thomas Gathright.

2. Legislation during the period immediately succeeding the Reconstruction carefully conserved the rights of the Negroes.

3. From the first there seems to have been in the minds of some a lack of faith in the capacity of the Negro to profit by instruction. In later days this sentiment found expression in the utterances of Vardaman and his followers.

4. Belief that industrial training offered the best form of education for Negroes became evident during the eighties, but it has never developed strength enough to bring about the adoption of the principle.

5. Among the leaders in later days, advocates for giving the Negro adequate educational opportunities have not been wanting. The most prominent spokesmen for the Negro's rights were Governors Longino and Noel, Superintendents Preston and Kincannon, and Bishop Galloway.

6. Although opposition to the prevailing form of education has apparently been the dominant political sentiment within recent years, radical action has in most cases been successfully combatted by a conservative majority.

7. White educators have generally favored providing adequate school facilities for Negroes.

8. The Negroes in early days were enthusiastic and eager to secure education. We have few expressions from them in recent years, but the impression one gets is that the masses have become apathetic.

III. *On account of the financial depression of the state, rapid educational progress was retarded until after 1900. Despite unfavorable conditions during certain periods, the efficiency of the white schools has slowly but steadily increased. The efficiency of Negro schools, on the other hand, has not improved, and even shows signs of retrogression.*

1. The efforts of the Reconstructionists resulted in the organization of a strong administrative machine, but one too expensive for a state in sore economic straits. To these efforts, however, is due the establishment of a large number of Negro schools.

2. The southern Democrats, after overthrowing the carpet-bag government, were forced to retrench along educational lines. Re-

trenchment resulted disastrously for both white and colored schools, but there was no direct move to deprive the Negro of the privileges of education.

3. During the first decade after the return to southern rule, the enrolment and average daily attendance increased rapidly, but the efficiency of the schools was of a very low order.

4. The reforms of 1886 gave the schools administrative machinery which has remained substantially unchanged until the present date. Statistics indicate very little progress in white schools from 1886 to 1900, yet considering the activity of the state department, there was probably internal progress which is not evident in the figures. Statistics indicate that Negro schools during this period were positively on the retrograde. The enrolment increased, but the average daily attendance and the number of teachers remained stationary. The number of pupils per teacher increased from 50.9 to 63.5, and the average monthly salary decreased about eight dollars.

5. The period from 1900 to 1910 is a period of marked prosperity for the white schools. A larger number of children were now being reached, and more efficient supervision, better teachers, and more comfortable buildings were now being provided. The Negro schools, however, show few signs of improvement. They have continued to be poorly equipped, poorly attended, and poorly taught.

6. The efficiency of Negro teachers, as represented by the grade of certificate held, has steadily declined since 1890. This has in part been due to the cutting off of the support of the Normal Department of Tougaloo University, and the closing of the Holly Springs State Normal.

7. Never directly, except in the case of the closing of the State Normal School, has the state discriminated against the Negro schools. A four-months' term is mandatory, and both white and colored children are to receive the benefit of the state school fund. The present plan of distributing the school fund has even worked in favor of the Negroes to the extent of providing comparatively high salaries for Negro teachers in the populous black counties. A county institute is provided for each race if the number of school districts for each race exceed fifteen.

Loopholes for discrimination by county authorities have been left, by permitting the county superintendents to fix the salaries of teachers within certain limits, and by basing the salary upon the grade of certificate awarded by the county examining board. Although under this law the salaries of white teachers have always been higher than those of colored teachers, it is impossible to tell to what extent discrimination has been practised, since county superintendents are required to take into consideration not only the grade of certificate, but also the average attendance, the ability of the teacher to manage the school, etc. The supply of teachers, and the differing social wants of the two races have doubtless helped to determine the salaries paid Negro teachers.

IV. *Lack of progress in education is paralleled by a lack of progress in the social and economic life of the Negro. The slender provision for education offered in the public schools has been insufficient to produce appreciable results. Besides, no attempt has been made to provide training suited to the needs of the colored race.*

1. As a rule, Negroes have been slow to acquire homes of their own, but in the cities of the state, where the schools are under the supervision of competent white superintendents, they have acquired homes more rapidly than elsewhere.

2. They have made little progress in the ownership of farm property and have not developed managerial ability to any extent. As an economic factor, the Negro farmer represents a very low degree of efficiency. With proper training along agricultural lines, however, he promises to make a much more efficient operative.

3. It can hardly be said that the education which has in past been provided, has directed any considerable number of Negroes into the professions, nor is it likely that the Negro will compete successfully in this field for some years to come.

4. Crime among Negroes is certainly on the increase. It cannot be declared that education is the cause of this, for many of the prisoners are illiterate. Besides, the schooling which has been provided has been scarcely sufficient to influence Negroes one way or the other. Further, defective home life, which criminologists agree upon as the chief cause for crime, is found to be a very significant factor among Mississippi Negroes. Proper training along moral and industrial lines alone will remedy the situation. To neglect to provide the necessary school facilities for development along these lines is itself a crime against society, and one which will result in the detriment of both white and colored races.

BIBLIOGRAPHY

PRIMARY SOURCES

STATE REPORTS, JOURNALS, STATISTICAL DATA, ETC.

1. Reports of the State Superintendent, 1870–1910.
2. Reports of the United States Commissioner of Education, 1870–1910.
3. Reports of the State Treasurer, 1872, 1874.
4. Reports of the State Auditor, 1874, 1876, 1886, 1889, 1900, 1901, 1903, 1905, 1907, 1909, 1910.
5. State Laws, 1845, 1865–1910.
6. House and Senate Journals, Messages of Governors, 1865–1910.
7. Journals of Constitutional Conventions, 1865, 1868, 1890.
8. Eleventh, Twelfth, and Thirteenth Censuses. Also Special Reports.
9. Freedmen's Bureau Reports, 1865–1869.
10. Proceedings of Peabody Fund Trustees, 1867–1900.
11. United States Congress, Report of Committee on Southern Affairs, 1872.
12. The Negro Year Book.

EDUCATIONAL LITERATURE

1. *Mississippi Educational Journal*, 1871.
2. *American Journal of Education*, 1875.
3. *The Mississippi Teacher*, 1888–1889.
4. *The Mississippi Journal of Education*, 1895.
5. Proceedings of Mississippi Teachers' Association, 1877, 1883, 1887, 1892, 1894, 1905, 1910.
6. Miscellaneous papers and pamphlets of Mission Boards doing work in the South.
7. Current Periodicals: *World's Work, Atlantic Monthly, South Atlantic Quarterly*, etc.

NEWSPAPERS

1. Vicksburg *Times*, 1868–1870.
2. Hinds County *Gazette*, 1870–1878, 1887–1891, 1903–1904.
3. *The Weekly Pilot*, 1875.
4. Port Gibson *Record* (*Reveille*), 1887–1890.
5. New Orleans *Times Democrat*, 1903.
6. Greenville *Democrat*, 1903.
7. Jackson *Daily News*, 1903.
8. *Daily Clarion*, Brookhaven *Ledger*, *Clarion-Ledger*, 1868 to the present.
9. Natchez *Democrat*, 1867–1873.

SECONDARY SOURCES

1. Publications of the Mississippi Historical Society, fifteen volumes.
2. Fleming: *Documentary History of Reconstruction,* two volumes.
3. Garner: *Reconstruction in Mississippi.*
4. Lynch: *The Facts of Reconstruction.*
5. *Memoirs of Mississippi,* Goodspeed's Edition.
6. Rowland: *Mississippi* (Encyclopedia).
7. Lowry and McCardle: *History of Mississippi.*
8. Riley: *School History of Mississippi.*
9. Eaton: *Grant, Lincoln, and the Freedmen.*
10. Pierce: *The Freedmen's Bureau.*
11. Fant: *Secondary Education in Mississippi* (New York University dissertation).
12. Beeson: *Die Organisation der Neger-erziehung in den Vereinigten Staaten von Amerika seit 1860* (Leipzig dissertation).
13. Stone: *Studies in the American Race Problem* (including studies by W. F. Wilcox).
14. Mayes: *History of Education in Mississippi.*

STATISTICAL SUMMARY

MISSISSIPPI SCHOOLS 1871 TO 1910

SCHOOL POPULATION, ENROLMENT, AND AVERAGE DAILY ATTENDANCE OF WHITE AND COLORED CHILDREN

	SCHOOL POPULATION[1]		ENROLMENT		AVERAGE DAILY ATTENDANCE	
Year	White	Colored	White	Colored	White	Colored
1871			66,257	45,429	49,290	36,040
1875	141,514	176,945	78,404	89,813	40,381	60,514
1876	171,147[2]	184,857[2]	76,026[2]	90,178[2]	65,384[3]	68,580[3]
1877	150,504[4]	174,485[4]	84,374	76,154	52,384[3]	44,627[3]
1878	155,679	190,211	101,201	104,177	64,318	71,608
1879	156,434	205,936	105,957	111,796	66,381	72,592
1880	175,251	251,438	112,944	123,710	72,881	83,880
1881	180,026	239,433	111,655	125,633	74,647	85,417
1882	185,026	259,105	104,451	109,630	61,738	73,578
1883	180,093	267,478	125,598	141,398	68,946	85,517
1884	185,026	259,105	129,647	149,373	85,294	99,127
1885			142,177	154,430	84,347	101,038
1886	202,532	369,090	129,203	153,530	84,884	99,134
1887	202,532	269,090	126,919	143,825	77,868	85,996
1888	196,247	268,100	147,817	162,304	89,933	94,085
1889	191,792	272,682	148,435	173,552	90,716	101,710
1890			150,868	183,290	96,077	111,627
1891	206,608	291,014	154,447	173,378	93,282	104,298
1892	214,419	301,764	161,986	178,941	96,818	100,457
1893			154,459	180,464	93,099	101,844
1894	220,751	320,780	158,685	186,899	98,753	107,494
1895	220,751	320,780	162,830	187,785	99,048	103,635

[1] School age is from five to twenty-one.
[2] "Approximately correct," says superintendent.
[3] Average monthly enrolment.
[4] "Estimate low," says superintendent.

MISSISSIPPI SCHOOLS 1871 TO 1910

SCHOOL POPULATION, ENROLMENT, AND AVERAGE DAILY ATTENDANCE OF WHITE AND COLORED CHILDREN (*Continued*)

	SCHOOL POPULATION		ENROLMENT		AVERAGE DAILY ATTENDANCE	
Year	White	Colored	White	Colored	White	Colored
1896	216,300[5]	315,000[5]	165,878	197,875		
1897	216,300[5]	315,000[5]	170,811	196,768		
1898						
1899			167,178[6]	191,968[6]	98,379[6]	102,447[6]
1900	227,470	331,330[7]				
1901			179,142	208,346	108,805	119,190
1902			185,214	213,961	111,034	113,919
1903			192,881	210,766	115,079	118,096
1904			200,365	233,612	114,781	123,390
1905			199,293	224,438	114,253	121,039
1906			209,752	243,676	125,295	142,602
1907			211,549	270,659	134,846	150,201
1908	301,548	410,089	205,978	278,713	122,261	137,197
1909			221,392	238,639	138,813	145,153
1910			224,837	244,300	118,541	142,834

[5] United States Commissioner's Report, 1895–1896.
[6] In reports from this date on, the statistics for separate districts are given separately. Figures here given are totals for rural and separate district schools.
[7] United States Commissioner's Report, school age, five to eighteen.

WHITE AND COLORED TEACHERS, AVERAGE MONTHLY
SALARIES 1875 TO 1910

	NUMBER OF TEACHERS		AVERAGE MONTHLY SALARIES	
Year	*White*	*Colored*	*White*	*Colored*
1875	2,859	2,109	$57.50[1]	$53.45[1]
1876	1,773[2]	1,005[2]	41.08	38.54
1877	2,669[3]	1,459[3]	29.19[2]	29.19[2]
1878	2,948	1,813	27.00	27.00[2]
1879	3,255	2,112	30.26	30.26
1880	3,255	2,314	30.05	30.05
1881	3,414	2,644	30.07	30.07
1882	2,910	2,272	30.03	30.03
1883	3,559	2,784	32.68	32.68
1884	3,873	2,933	28.73	28.73
1885	4,215[4]	3,134[4]	28.74	28.74
1886	3,840	3,012	31.37	27.40
1887	3,421	2,592	34.44	25.24
1888	3,643	2,826	34.52	24.05
1889	4,018	3,097	33.97	24.16
1890	4,269	3,222	33.37	23.20
1891	4,334	3,212	32.41	22.54
1892	4,634	3,288	32.33	24.52
1893	4,296	2,201	30.45	22.31
1894	4,385	3,192	33.04	21.46
1895	4,591	3,264	33.04	21.53
1896				
1897	4,747[5]	3,156[5]		

[1] Superintendent Cardoza said that varying salaries for races for this year were due to the fact that a greater number of white males taught schools for both races than did colored males—Superintendent's Report, 1876, p. 13.

[2] United States Commissioner's Report, 1880, p. 176.

[3] Ten counties not reported.

[4] Figures unreliable.

[5] United States Commissioner's Report, 1897.

WHITE AND COLORED TEACHERS, AVERAGE MONTHLY
SALARIES 1875 TO 1910 (*Continued*)

	NUMBER OF TEACHERS		AVERAGE MONTHLY SALARIES	
Year	*White*	*Colored*	*White*	*Colored*
1898				
1899	4,419	3,023		
1900				
1901	5,147[6]	3,368[6]	$30.64	$19.39
1902	5,159[7]	3,472[7]	31.48	19.66
1903	5,524[6]	3,398[6]	33.85[8]	19.69[8]
1904	5,740[6]	3,562[6]		
1905	5,774[6]	3,559[6]	38.90[8]	20.83[8]
1906	5,868[6]	3,614[6]		
1907	5,981[9]	3,518[9]		
1908	5,850[6]	3,596[6]		
1909	6,099[6]	3,552	41.49[8]	20.31[8]
1910	6,472[6]	3 692[6]	42.38[8]	20.52[8]

[6] Teachers in both separate district and rural schools.

[7] 807 teachers in separate districts, added by author to figures for rural schools; 507 to the number for whites, and 300 to the colored.

[8] Salaries for teachers in rural schools.

[9] United States Commissioner's Report, 1907.